This book is property of
The Angel Inn.

To purchase a copy please
enquire at reception.

From a watercolour by John Strickland Goodall (1908-96), HVA

Crosstracks to Hindon

Richard Dewhurst

First published in the United Kingdom in 2005 by
The Hobnob Press, PO Box 1838, East Knoyle, Salisbury SP3 6FA
in association with Hindon Parish Council

British Library Cataloguing in Publication Data
A catalogue record for this book is available from the British Library.

The watercolour painting used on the front cover and as the frontispiece, by John Strickland Goodall (1908-96), was given by the artist in 1956 to Hindon Women's Institute and is now in Hindon Village Archives. It is used with the owners' kind permission, and by courtesy of Felix Rosenstiel's Widow & Son Ltd., London. Back cover. Photo: author 2002

ISBN 0-946418-33-0

Typeset in 11.5/16 pt Georgia
Typesetting and origination by John Chandler
Printed in Great Britain by Salisbury Printing Company Ltd, Salisbury

Contents

Common Abbreviations

Cal. Chart. Calendar of Charter Rolls, PRO
Cal. Pat.   Calendar of Patent Rolls, PRO
CUP   Cambridge University Press
DNB   Dictionary of National Biography
GR   Ordnance Survey grid reference
HMSO   HM Stationery Office
HRO   Hampshire Record Office, Winchester
HVA   Hindon Village Archives
LTA   Land Tax assessment
NMR   National Monuments Record (of English Heritage), Swindon
OS   Ordnance Survey
OUP   Oxford University Press
PCC   Parochial Church Council
PRO   Public Record Office; from 2003 The National Archives, Kew
SMR   Sites & Monuments Record (Wilts. C.C. Archaeologist, Trowbridge)
VCH/W   Victoria County History, Wilts.
WANHM   *Wiltshire Archaeological & Natural History Magazine*
WANHS   Wiltshire Archaeological & Natural History Society, Devizes
WSRO   Wiltshire & Swindon Record Office, Trowbridge
WTA   Window Tax assessment

Introduction and Acknowledgements

The first local attempt to collect material for a history of Hindon and nearby villages seems to have been made by Edward Jerrim (1888-1962), journalist and accountant, who had worked in Nigeria and settled in the village in 1920. While working in London on a west African newspaper in the 1930s he spent time in the Public Record Office noting hundreds of its references to this area, and meticulously indexing his results. A serving soldier in both world wars who subsequently busied himself in Hindon parochial duties, he did not live to work his notes into a history. They have been extensively used here.

Subsequent research and inquiries by others eventually bore fruit in Norah Sheard's *The History of Hindon* in 1979. It was written before the appearance of the section on Hindon in the Victoria County History and missed some earlier sources. It contains much detail, sometimes disordered; its great drawback from the point of view of subsequent researchers is a huge lack of references to earlier sources quoted. It is still of value on the transition to the modern village, a part of which section is quoted here.

For 2000 Hindon Parochial Church Council commissioned the present writer's *The Church in Hindon* to mark the millennium. Published by Rupert Attlee (Hindon Publishing) it traces the development of the faith in the area from earliest times. It contains detail on liturgical aspects and on church buildings that are mostly not repeated here.

In 2001 Hindon Parish Council recognised a need from local residents and visitors for an up-to-date history that has resulted in the present work. Such have to be partly community projects. I can count well over 30 local people who have contributed with reminiscences, letters, loans of photographs and books, opinions, papers, advice, transcriptions of texts, typing, ground surveys, internet inquiries, e-mail support and photo enhancement. There is no space to list them all here; they know who they are and I thank them all sincerely. Where appropriate, providers of specific information are named in the text or notes; a name accompanied by further qualification denotes a present or past local resident.

In alphabetical order, thanks are especially due to Heather Bull, Jerrim's daughter, whose long memory and careful collection of notes, cuttings and records have been invaluable. To Roy Canham, County Archaeologist, whose interest in and advice on the local prehistoric archaeology has opened exciting prospects for future inquiry. Philippa Cawthorne's 2000 MA thesis on Hindon's economic history 1700-1850, referenced below, considerably reduced my need to rootle out references and will be a valuable addition to the village archives. My publisher, Dr. John Chandler, has unrivalled local knowledge and has been generous with advice, encouragement and corrections. Clare, Lady Margadale played a significant role in the preparation of Sheard's book, notably in the discovery and acquisition of the Calthorpe map (q.v.), an essential source. She has here again provided encouragement and support, notably with information on the Morrison family and aspects of local topography. Dr. Lorna Haycock, Sandell Librarian of WANHS in Devizes and staff have, as ever, been paragons of helpfulness, as have staff of the county record office in Trowbridge and local studies libraries. Roddy McColl enhanced eight of the photographs reproduced here, with brilliant results.

But without the speed and accuracy of Kay Maycock's typing there is no doubt that my task would have been greatly prolonged, and tiresome.

Richard Dewhurst
25th February
2005

THIS WORK IS DEDICATED TO THE MEMORY OF BISHOP PETER DES ROCHES, WITHOUT WHOM THERE WOULD HAVE BEEN NO REASON TO WRITE IT

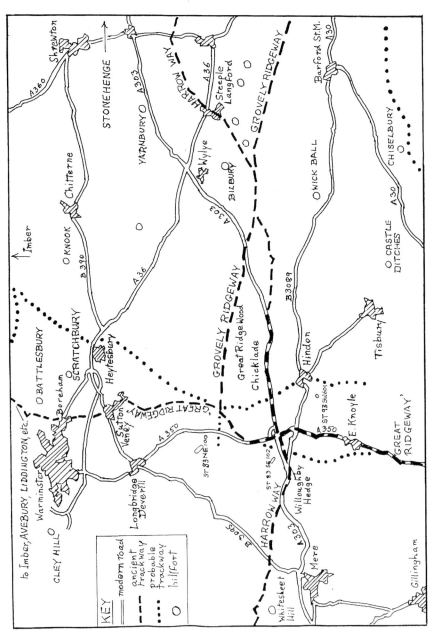

Plate 1. Prehistoric trackways and monuments in the Hindon area

Beginnings

Hindon's position on or near dominant east-west routes has largely determined its success or failure across time, and its occasional witness of national events. Plate 1 shows, in simplified form the relationship of modern roads to some probable prehistoric trackways in the area. The best known is in fact not east–west but north–south, but originally perhaps most significant. Called the 'Great Ridgeway' by Timperley and Brill,[1] it starts at the Goring/ Streatley crossing of the Thames where it picks up various old tracks coming from East Anglia via Ivinghoe Beacon. It follows the northern edge of the Berkshire and Marlborough Downs via Uffington (White Horse Hill), Liddington and Barbury, passing close by Avebury at West Overton; turns south across Pewsey Vale and traverses Salisbury Plain via Imber; and probably crossing the River Wylye at Boreham, passes Sutton Veny. Via Littlecombe Hill (GR ST 896399) it takes a turn to the west and probably follows roughly the line of the present A350 from Pertwood to Shaftesbury, subsequently wandering down to the Devon coast, perhaps at Seaton, near Lyme Regis. One of several subsidiary tracks (shown by the dotted line on Pl.1) probably led from near Botley Oak Brake (GR ST 898365) south through Hindon. This later formed the basis of its High Street. For the purposes of this study let us call it Ridgeway/H.

Timperley and Brill are not the only people who have attempted to trace the route of this ancient highway, and acknowledge that the effort 'must be eked out with theory, conjecture and imagination'. They are, however a good starting point. Their placing of the main route in the Hindon area, or indeed elsewhere, should not be confused with what Ordnance Survey (OS) Landranger and Explorer maps now call the Wessex Ridgeway. This is a designated and signposted footpath for walkers. It has to avoid busy main roads and army training areas, and it deviates markedly from the 'Great Ridgeway', including around Hindon.[2]

The Harroway or Hardway ran from Dover through Farnham, Surrey; the Stonehenge complex; Steeple Langford and, briefly following the line of the present A303 at Chicklade, descended via Whitesheet Hill (GR ST 803350) into Somerset.

The track here called the Grovely Ridgeway, also starting on the Kent coast, led via Wilton on to Great Ridge and so to the Mendips and the Bristol Channel.

Nobody can date these routes with any precision, but their obvious connection of the great Neolithic and Bronze Age funerary and religious centres of Avebury and Stonehenge suggest that they, or parts of them, go back many thousands of years. Such tracks are likely to have marginally shifted sideways over time as old alignments became impassable through wear, or when lower summer routes were used, but the basic routings could have been used by traders and pedlars before settled societies solidified. It is striking how many terminate in southern and south-western coastal harbours, signifying substantial trade with the continent long before the Romans came. For example, Hengistbury Head, sheltering Christchurch harbour, flourished in the late Iron Age, doing considerable trade, particularly in wine imports, from Armorica (Brittany). A trackway connected it with Blandford.[3]

For simplicity, Pl.1 omits all but three of the more than 100 barrows of one sort or another identified in this landscape, (many more have long disappeared). There is a particularly dense cluster west of the Deverills and on Whitesheet Hill.[4]

The first barrow, designated SMR no. ST83 NE100,[5] is the well preserved Neolithic long barrow 3½ miles NE of Hindon on Summerslade Down (GR ST 872375). It has not been excavated, but suggests the presence of a significant and stable community of the earliest farmers, maybe five or six thousand years ago. On the analogy of excavations of the West Kennett long barrow near Avebury it seems that the bodies of significant individuals in its society may have been exposed and the bones later collected in such tombs, marking the edges of a tribal territory, as if to say to strangers 'This is our land, guarded by our ancestors'. There is a much smaller, more eroded long barrow (SMR no. ST83 SE102) near the A303/A350 crossing, emphatically not to be examined while driving east on the A303. It is impossible to say what Hindon's place might have had to do with all of this, except that this general area was occupied by the earliest herdsmen and primitive agriculturalists from time out of mind.

Most of the said 100-plus barrows are round (*tumuli* on OS maps) and belong to the Bronze Age (say 2500 to *c*.800BC). These

Plate 2. Bronze Age bowl barrow ST93 SW601. Hindon church spire can just be seen, extreme right [Photo: author]

are tombs of the rich and powerful, sometimes warrior chiefs buried with their accoutrements, and speak of a very different and more stratified society than the Neolithic. Let us consider just one, SMR no. ST93 SW601 at GR 903322 (Pl. 2). This, well known to Hindon dog-walkers, was once one of a cluster of perhaps three barrows and a number of field marks that have now been ploughed flat. It is described as a 'bowl barrow', 20 paces in diameter and 4½ feet high with a central collapse that probably reflects a robbery in antiquity. There is other evidence of field systems to its south.

This suggests a significant Bronze Age community centred only one mile from the present middle of Hindon, existing over several generations. It must add to the puzzle of whether anything existed in Hindon before its 1220 foundations as a borough, a puzzle to which we shall return.

There are also remains of about 16 hillforts from the Iron Age (*c.*800BC to the Roman period) within 10 miles.[6] Some are shown in Pl.1. These may be fortifications, or enclosures with other purposes, of the tribe that the Romans later called Durotriges (their own, Celtic name for themselves is unknown). They, loosely centred in Dorset but extending into south Wiltshire, subsequently offered stiff resistance to the Roman invasion.[7]

Romans

The Romans seem unlikely to have made any particular impact on Hindon's site itself, but it does lie within three miles or so of two early Roman roads.

The invasion of south Britain ordered by the Emperor Claudius in AD 43 involved four legions whose initial deployments are not entirely clear and cause much disagreement among experts and theorists. The subjugation of the Durotriges may have begun with a thrust from Kent or possibly with a second landing on the south coast near the Isle of Wight, probably by Legio II Augusta led by the future emperor Vespasian. There was tough defence at several hillforts, notably the colossal 'Maiden Castle' at Dorchester, a siege graphically revealed by Sir Mortimer Wheeler's excavations in the late 1930s.

What is certain is that a fortress was established at Lake Farm, near the Iron Age fort of Badbury Rings, north of Poole Harbour. In due course a road was built by military engineers NNW to Aquae Sulis (Bath), at its start in more or less a straight line in that unlovable way of Roman road builders. Although Bath had a spring sacred to the Celtic goddess Sulis long before the Romans arrived, the purpose of this road was clearly strategic in that the first phase of the invasion drew breath on the line of the later Fosse Way built from Devon to Lincoln. Bath lies close by its course.[1]

This road's route is clear enough until near Shaftesbury, but becomes hard to follow in the lumpy country around the Donheads.

Traces of it were found just east of Knoyle during sewerage works in 1972, and confirmed in 1995 during grading for the by-pass of the village by the A350. A Romano-British cemetery is said to lie close by, and coins from the 1st to the late 4th century have been found.[2]

The second road ran from Sorviodunum, which we now call Old Sarum, to the already-worked lead mines in the Mendip Hills in Somerset, which the Romans are known to have been developing only six years after their invasion landings, needing the metal to make pewter, and for their coffins and drains. Its route is uncertain for much of its course, but can be traced rising from Wilton through Grovely Wood on to Great Ridge, where it follows the basic line of the old Grovely Ridgeway (Pl.1). The nearest point to Hindon is in Great Ridge Wood, and accurately marked on OS Explorer map 143. The *agger* (raised embankment on which the metalled surface was once laid) can just be found in sapling trees south of the big east–west firebreak, with which the Roman route has sometimes been confused (GR ST 929362). It can be traced again just north of Lower Pertwood Farm going towards Warminster on the A350, before it takes a crooked line over the folded country towards Monkton Deverill.[3] Roman engineers could sometimes be lovable.

Just outside Hindon to the west is a series of old cultivation terraces, from Hawking Down towards Two Mile Down (Pl.3). The Wiltshire County Archaeologist viewed these in 2003 and said that they looked far too long and bold in section for the prehistoric, and that they suggest late Romano-British cultivation. He observed that they closely resemble in scale those on Chapperton Down, near Tilshead (GR ST 002481), which are associated with clear evidence of a Romano-British village, presumably of estate workers.

In the 4th century AD the Empire in the west largely recovered from previous disasters, and for Britain it was an agricultural golden age. Improvements in farming economics and techniques under the management of large villa-estates led to a huge increase in grain production that not only fed the local military and civilian

Plate 3. Probable late Roman cultivation terraces on Two Mile Down
[Photo: author]

population but produced a surplus to export to Gaul when barbarian invasions there disrupted agriculture.[4] Several such estates and their villas have in recent years been found on the edges of Salisbury Plain; the most striking recent excavation has been on the hill above Bradford-on-Avon.

Our local terraces, close to two Roman roads, offer an exciting prospect if supporting evidence, such as finds, can substantiate this theory. We need a village, or still better a villa.

Saxons

The early Saxons are not known for their record keeping skills, and the date when they first arrived in this immediate area (after their first infiltration into south and east England in the late 5th and early 6th centuries AD), as well as the progress of Christian missionizing here after the first landing of Augustine in Thanet in AD 597 will always be obscure to us.[1]

Equally obscure are the nature and timing of the end of Roman imperial administration in Britain. Between, say, 409 and 425 units of the garrison probably tramped away in response to various imperatives elsewhere, no doubt swiftly followed by imperial civil servants.[2] Towns would have fallen into local control, but the old roads would still have remained in comparatively good order for some time. The Roman road from Badbury Rings was probably one. Several field names in Knoyle still have likely Saxon origins, and two Saxon field charters of 947 and 956 refer to the territory as *Cnugel*. They define its boundaries with West Knoyle, but whether *Cnugel's* limits extended to the present Hindon is unknown. Masonry on the north wall of the church of St. Mary's at Knoyle and a very worn churchyard cross are believed to be of Saxon origin.[3]

And Hindon? We don't know, but the place-name is clearly Saxon. It first appears in written form as *Hinedon* much later in account rolls of the see of Winchester in the early 13th century. It also gets named as *Hynedon, Hyndon, Esthindon, Hyndoun, Hindon Strete, Hendon* and even *Hindon*. This does not matter.

Spelling of English remained pretty ramshackle until the late 18th century.

Eminent scholars have told us that the *don* element comes from Old English (OE) *dun*, meaning a hill or down. They speculate that probably the element *hin* derives from *higna*, genitive plural of an OE word meaning a household, ecclesiastical or secular. If so, this could suggest that in Saxon times there was some sort of building here, or that somebody lived here who belonged to a household elsewhere. (A second piece of evidence to bring to the puzzle mentioned in 'Beginnings'). They note that in neighbouring Fonthill there is record of one Aethelm Higa, who 'clearly' belonged to such a household, possibly to that of Alfred the Great himself (reigned 871-899) at his estate at Wardour.[4] Maybe so, but these theories have been distorted by several writers who should know better to imply that Hindon's name is derived from a hill nearby called *higna dun*. This is stretching interpretation a bit far.

Alfred, however, did play a major role in this landscape. After his surprise by Guthrum and his Danes at Chippenham at Christmas 877 he retreated to Athelney in the Somerset marshes (where he certainly did not burn cakes). In May 878 he summoned the *fyrd* of Somerset, Wiltshire and west Hampshire to meet at *Ecgbrihtesstan* (Egbert's Stone) for his grudge match against Guthrum.[5] Its location has been variously put at Alfred's Tower, Coombe Street, Willoughby Hedge and Kingston Deverill, where King Egbert was said to have held a court.[6] The army crossed the Plain to fall on and rout the Danes at *Ethandun*, probably on the downs above Edington. This presage to a turning point in English history would just not have been witnessed by somebody hanging about where Hindon now is.

There is another piece of evidence about this place. Some of the best sources on Saxon occupation are their charters of land ownership and boundaries. The present Hindon's SE corner was touched by the northern boundary of land-holding of *Tissesburgh*

(Tisbury), an estate probably originally granted by Alfred to his daughter Aethelgifu, the first abbess of Shaftesbury, in about 888. It was a large estate that then stretched to Ansty in the S, Sedgehill in the W, and Sutton Mandeville in the E. This grant was later confirmed by Aethelred II, the 'Unready', probably without major amendments, in a charter of 984.

This document traces the NE boundary of that estate from the present Fonthill Lake on to the present B3089 towards Hindon, but forking left at the house now called The Needles on to the green lane that comes out at the foot of Hindon High Street, '*on þone herpoð*' (on to the herepath).

The meaning of this strange word herepath has been disputed by scholars, but probably means some sort of a Saxon military road. The *here* element clearly relates to the German *herren*, which can mean men, or people, or even warriors. This need not mean that herepaths were tramped by vast armies; indeed in Saxon-speak three dozen men could have been called an army. They could merely have been protected trackways used by royal patrols or officials.

R.H. Jackson, the latest surveyor of these boundaries, has this to say about this herepath, which he traces coming down to Hindon's High Street from Tisbury:

> Before the making of Hindon High Street [c.1220] this road followed the present School Lane which I believe was continuous with the road N of it that leads to Chicklade. That being so, the junction with the Herepath was either where the [green lane already mentioned] meets the Tisbury to Hindon road, or where the stream [the Dene] meets School Lane . . . The School Lane going N is cut off by the present Hindon to Berwick road [B3089] from another road a short distance to its W which leads N to Chicklade. These two sections, once joined, I suggest, constituted the ancient Herepath, which climbs steadily, crosses the old Ox Drove, and drops down a steeper slope to meet and cross over the A303 . . . at the W end of Chicklade village.[7]

And where then? If one continues north and veers right a bit one comes to the western end of Grovely Grim's Ditch, a bank-and-ditch feature that runs for about nine miles from near Wilton up on to the Great Ridge. Its origin and purpose is very obscure but some authorities think that it is post-Roman. Could it be that it is a Saxon boundary mark to which the herepath led?

A ghost of the herepath survived until at least the 15th century, when a field called *Herpethakere* is listed in a register of charters and property.[8]

Normans

The Norman conquest of 1066 brought a radical change in the ownership of the manor of East Knoyle, known to the Saxons as *Cnugel,* which by this time clearly included the place that we now know as Hindon. It had been a royal manor in the days of Aethelred II (reigned 978-1016).[1] In the time of Edward the Confessor (reigned 1042-1066) it was held by the lady Aeleva. This was the largest Wiltshire estate in lay hands other than those of the king and members of the house of Godwin. Aeleva probably also rented the manor of Chalke and a 10-hide estate in Berkshire.[2]

After the Conquest Aeleva was dispossessed and the estate granted by William I to William fitz Osbern, one of the battle-hardened lords who fought with him at Hastings and who brought to the battle and paid for substantial contingents of knights. It was, in one way, a commercial venture that paid off. Fitz Osbern became the king's seneschal, was created Earl of Hereford, a vital border fiefdom, and acted as a regent when the king felt secure enough to revisit Normandy in 1067. After signal service to the new regime in England, he was killed in 1071 when involved in a dynastic dispute in Flanders, then allied to Normandy. His son Earl Roger de Breteuil became involved in a foolish and futile revolt against King William in 1075, was stripped of his earldom and all his lands, though happily not of his head. The estate of East Knoyle reverted to the king.[3]

That was the situation when, after his Christmas court at Gloucester in December 1085, 21 months before his death, William held deep speech with his council about this land, how it was peopled, and with what sort of men. He sent his men all over England into every shire to ascertain . . . [how much each landowner held, and from whom].[4]

Everyone held land directly or indirectly from the king, the apex of the feudal hierarchy. He wished to know what he was worth. The great Domesday survey that eventually resulted was not a census – it gives us no figures of population. It is all about land; it is a tax assessment and a fixing of land rights to guide subsequent legal administration.[5]

This is what it says about East Knoyle (*Chenvel*) :

The King holds *Chenvel*. Aeleva held it in the time of King Edward. It paid *geld* (tax) on 30 hides. Land for 15 ploughs. In lordship 17½ hides. 5 ploughs; 10 slaves.

16 villagers, 10 smallholders and 18 cottagers with 10 ploughs. Meadow, 15 acres; pasture 1 league long and ½ league wide; woodland ½ league long and as wide.

The value was £28; now £30.

Gilbert has 1 hide of this land. 3 smallholders are there. Value 7s 6d.[6]

It is not easy to interpret this ancient description of landholdings, particularly in the case of 'hides'. Originally the hide was the basic Anglo-Saxon land division sufficient to support the average peasant, but it varied geographically and according to the productivity of the land. Nationally records are pretty scant, and it seems we shall all be long gone before scholars are agreed on how many acres went to a hide in any one area. In Wessex a figure of 40 is often given, but where such documents as Domesday give any correlation a lower and variable figure seems to emerge.[7] We cannot therefore say how much of Knoyle manor was cultivated, or whether this extended to what is now Hindon on its edge. A league was a variable measure, usually from three to five miles; we do not know what it comprised here.

There also exist three copies of a separate contemporary survey made of the south-western counties and bits of Wiltshire that has become known as the Exon or Exeter Domesday. It places *Chenvel* in the hundred of Mere (see below for hundreds), and confirms that the king owned 17½ hides directly. However it adds the names of others who held parcels of land, presumably from the king. They are the Abbot of Glastonbury, the Abbess of Wilton, Walter Giffard, Gilbert Maminot and Godric the huntsman. This is difficult to reconcile with the Exchequer version, but it gives us more early names associated with the Knoyle area.[8]

In 1088 William II gave the Knoyle estate to Henry de Beaumont, Earl of Warwick. In 1184 the bishops of Winchester bought it from his grandson William, a transaction that was disputed, and not finally settled until 1204.[9] It then became known as Bishop's Knoyle or Knoyle Episcopi. The see's title was confirmed by Edward I in 1284,[10] and by Edward II in 1317.

Founder

Things now begin to get interesting, and specific to Hindon. Some time between 1206 and 1219 the then bishop of Winchester, Peter des Roches, decided, possibly when passing through Hindon, that this was the place for a market town.

Bishop Sir Peter des Roches, or de Rochys, or in Latin texts Petrus de Rupibus, was a native of Poitou, south of the Loire, or Anjou, north of it, both then part of the possessions of the English crown in France. He there entered the entourage of Richard Coeur de Lion, and served him as knight and clerk – this term presumably implying minor holy orders. He became a chamberlain at his court. When Richard died in 1199 he transferred his allegiance to King John and continued steadfastly in his service. John lost Normandy to the French in 1204 and des Roches, together with many other nobles and crown servants who lost estates and positions there, came to England with the king. They had nothing to lose, and John clung to these people, whom he clearly saw as a link to a province that he might one day recover. Des Roches became a close friend, confidant and general fixer for the king.

In reward for diplomatic services, John in 1205 sponsored des Roches's election to the bishopric of Winchester, second only to Canterbury in wealth and importance. This was only about 30 years after the great dispute between John's father Henry II and Thomas Becket about the judicial interface between king and church. Peter's election, by the Winchester chapter, was disputed, some preferring the dean. It shows the influence of the papacy over local churches in those days that this conflict had to go to the Pope for decision, and both candidates had to traipse to Rome for it (for decency's sake at different times and by different routes). Down through France, into Italy, to take lodgings in Rome to await the papal summons. When it came our Peter won the election, and was consecrated bishop by Pope Innocent III in September 1205. Then they had to come all the way back again.

What a picture this gives us of medieval Europe! A constant stream of messengers, officials, envoys, papal legates, pilgrims, supplicants, candidates, even kings going up and down the old Roman roads radiating from the Eternal City to all parts of Christian Europe.

The new bishop put part of the great resources of his see at the service of the king, and played a major role in the administration of the court and exchequer. He supported John in the later struggle with Innocent over church appointments. He held the office of Chief Justiciar of England in 1214–15, a post combining legal and administrative duties that left him as virtual regent in charge of the realm when John went a-campaigning in France.[1]

In the struggles with the northern barons that led to the signing of the first Magna Carta in 1215 des Roches advised John to concede and seems to have caused the administration to keep its part of the bargain. Not so the barons (none of whom features in history outside this episode). They had invited a French army into the south-east and East Anglia under the rather tentative command of Louis, son of King Philip Augustus of France, and they remained under arms after the settlement. The barons' only real motive was clearly to get rid of John.

Things were taken out of their hands when John died suddenly in October 1216. His supporters gathered at Gloucester and it was des Roches, one of John's executors, who as senior bishop present placed a plain gold circlet on the head of John's son, the nine-year-old Henry III, the royal regalia not being to hand (it was in the Wash). He became the boy's guardian and tutor.

There followed a remarkable feat of arms. In 1217 the French and rebel barons were occupying the town of Lincoln and besieging the castle in its NW corner, held by the loyal Nicolaa de la Hay, its hereditary chatelaine. Bishop Peter was one of the captains of a royalist force that marched to relieve her. The castle lay fast against the old Roman wall of Lindum, and so could be got into without entering the medieval town. Three of the leaders did so, and it was des Roches who made a quiet solo recce and spotted a blocked-up doorway into the space between castle and cathedral where the rebels were milling about. The troops were brought up, the gate was demolished, the royalists irrupted into the town, eventually scattering the French and capturing 300 knights with, it is said, no loss to the home team. Apart from a subsequent sea fight off Sandwich, this was effectively the end of Louis' occupation.

Plate 4. Effigy in Winchester Cathedral of Bishop Peter des Roches, founder of Hindon [reproduced by permission of the Dean and Chapter]

Peter had a long subsequent career, including participation in the Sixth Crusade, European diplomacy and an administration in the 1230s, surrounded by a coterie of Poitevin friends and relations. He died in 1238; his tomb is in Winchester Cathedral (Pl. 4).

Let us, however leave Peter's career at this moment of triumph. This formidable warrior priest was typical of those bishops who, since the Conqueror's time, tended to be good businessmen trained in the king's service and, owing their appointment to him, could be expected loyally to devote at least as much time to that service as to their spiritual duties. Des Roches, not at all English, cultivated, subtle, arrogant, was a ruthlessly efficient administrator and consequently deeply unpopular in some quarters (scurrilous verses about him were at one time circulated in London). There seems no good reason to doubt his conventional piety. He was an assiduous founder of churches and religious houses in England and the Holy Land, and paid much attention to the prosperity of his bishopric.[2]

Which brings us to Hindon.

Foundation – market . . .

The creation of new market towns (and fairs) was a dominant feature of the fledgling English economy in the 12th and 13th centuries. Kings retained the right to charter (license) such markets and to ensure that their charters were granted on an equitable basis; that markets were spaced far enough apart so as not to injure neighbouring arrangements. This distance varied according to conditions, but might be 6–8 miles, a third of a day's journey on foot. The purpose, in the days before permanent shops in country districts (our familiar village store only dates from well into the 19th century) was to create a weekly focus for the sale of essential supplies and produce, some of which, as in Hindon's case, would be grown on the plots of the stallholders. The king granted, for a fee, a charter to a person or a body that became the market owner, and theoretically could levy toll, a common tax on sales and purchases whether they took place in markets and fairs or on highways and bridges. One of the purposes of concentrating trade in markets was to facilitate the collection of toll.[1] But wait.

In the high middle ages the see of Winchester owned over 40 estates, mostly in Hampshire, but also stretching from Oxfordshire to the Isle of Wight and from Southwark to the rich estate of Taunton Deane in the west. Not all of these lay within the ecclesiastical jurisdiction of the bishopric. Des Roches founded or tried to revive five towns with markets between 1200 and 1220. He must have learned the economics of it when working for Richard I in

France early in his career. Richard was not just a dumb crusader; most of his non-crusading time was spent in Gascony, where he founded at least three market towns. Des Roches later hosted King John on Winchester manors at Downton, Knoyle and Taunton (where the bishops owned the castle), and would have been well aware that Hindon lay at the requisite distance from market centres like Mere and Shaftesbury, and as near as possible to the villages of the upper Nadder valley and those lying on the Wylye between Warminster and Wilton.[2]

This, perhaps gives us a clue as to the reason for Hindon's foundation. The likely route of a bishop's safari from Winchester to Taunton would be more or less on an east to west line, but making a kink to the north below Salisbury to take in Downton; along the approximate route of the present B3089 to rest at Knoyle; thereafter on the approximate A303 line, perhaps deviating to visit his manor at Rimpton in Somerset *en route* to Taunton.[3]

It is pleasant to imagine Bishop Peter, with his entourage of companions, clerks, chaplains, servants, grooms and protective men-at-arms halted in this place by one of those sudden downpours so well known to residents of the Dene, at the lowest point of the village, in recent years. While his flunkeys scurry for cover, he looks about him with his cool soldier's eye for country and notes that the rush of water down what is now the High Street could take wells to stem the flow. A fantasy? Not a bit of it. The account rolls of the bishopric (in the HRO at Winchester) are one of the best preserved medieval estate records in Europe, and they note that in 1220-1 the bishop paid for the sinking of a well of 14 fathoms (84 feet), cost 21 shillings, and for a rope and iron-bound bucket, 1 shilling. Maurice Beresford, the great historian of new town development, optimistically comments, 'Like Truth, it (the bucket) may one day be found at the bottom of the well.'[4]

Ridgeway/H was probably straightened, and the new town laid out across a wide street (now the High Street), running NW from the

Dene at the bottom of the present village. The width gave room for the tenants of the dwellings lining the street to erect stalls in front of them. Behind ran narrow burgage plots where they could grow their produce. Between groups of these ran lanes giving access to the fields beyond, like the bones of a kipper. Despite divisions and infillings in the intervening centuries (many houses today in the lower west High Street are separated from their small gardens) the resident or visitor today may still walk the street and see the fossilized ground plan of a small medieval new town. A footpath (Back Way) still runs behind the old burgage plots on the west side almost the whole length of the High Street. Had Hindon continued to develop and expand as Salisbury did, Back Way would have become a new street, and plots the other side of it would eventually have produced a grid plan, as at Salisbury. The comparison is not idle. The year 1220 is, of course, exactly the time that Bishop Poore of Salisbury got papal permission to move his seat from the hill now called Old Sarum to the river meadows where the cathedral now stands. Hindon was bang up to date.

The account rolls of the bishopric record that on foundation a croft and a *virgate* (a quarter-hide) of land rented by Roger de Hinedon and half a *virgate* rented by Ada de Hinedon had been deleted from the rent roll of Bishop's Knoyle and 'taken into demesne.'[5] This means that the status of the smallholding/s that they occupied had been changed, and that the bishop forewent the rent paid by Roger and Ada to his reeve at Knoyle because their land became part of the new market plantation. Whether they were dispossessed we do not know, but this is the third piece of evidence to add to that of the long-ago closeness of the Bronze Age settlement and the derivation of Hindon's place name (and, if you like, the fact that the Saxon herepath did not follow the line of the High Street) to suggest that there may have been an occasional building on the site before the foundation, but no more.

The account rolls do not record the names of the first burgage holders.[6] They would probably have paid rent (sixpence a year in

1224-5) for an empty plot; the erection of a building would probably have been their responsibility.[7] But there were advantages. The see paid for the well and a primitive market hall at the crossroads. As early as 1224 Henry III granted Hindon residents (but not visiting traders) exemption from toll, an edict confirmed by Richard II in 1393.[8] Soon after foundation the bishop conveyed to some burgesses plots of land outside the burgage area to ensure the settlement's survival.[9]

The market was successful, but initially not spectacularly so. Once the first recruitment of tenants was achieved, its proceeds for the bishops were £10 a year, whereas their rural manor of Knoyle pulled about £100.[10] There were 150 houses in c.1250, 77 poll tax payers in 1377.[11] Burgage tenure gave tenants the right to sell, exchange, or will their property, a right denied to manorial tenants. So the market gradually expanded, probably the whole length of the present High Street. It is likely that most of the inhabitants supported themselves from trade. In 1558 the town was said to abound in artisans.[12] There must have been providers of supplies for those who did not feed themselves, and bakers and brewers for those attending the market from other villages. John Aubrey, the 17th-century antiquary, rated it second in Wiltshire only to Warminster as a corn market,[13] and Blome's *Guidebook to Wiltshire* of 1673 describes in the same terms, 'very considerable', the markets of Salisbury, Warminster, Westbury, Devizes, Marlborough and Hindon.

Traders clearly did well enough to enable them to be generous. In about 1636 an agreement was made among farmers and maltsters using the markets of Hindon and Warminster that

> out of charity they would sell one bushel of barley at 4 shillings for one poor for every quarter they exposed for sale. Justices ordered in January 1647/8 that no maltster or barley buyer shall henceforth contract in these towns for any barley until sellers have deducted one bushel according to agreement.[14]

Thursday was always market day in Hindon. Peter des Roches was partly responsible in his years in power for enforcing nationally an earlier, largely disregarded, royal edict that markets should be held on weekdays, so that everyone could worship on Sundays.[15] In earlier times Sunday was often market day, the only time the poor peasants were free from toil to buy or sell necessities. How they fitted this in after enforcement of the edict is, of course, not recorded, but Bishop Peter fixed Hindon's (and Downton's) market on a Thursday and, as we shall see, there it always remained.

. . . and Fair

If markets were weekly events to facilitate the exchange of commodities and produce in a countryside without shops, fairs served a wider purpose. They were subjected to the same regulation by medieval kings, but were usually annual or biannual events lasting from one to three days. They drew trade from wider catchment areas and differing environments.

Hindon's fair was first granted by Henry III (des Roches no doubt guiding his infant fist) in 1219. The actual document has not survived. A square was laid out that offered more space for it than did the High Street for the weekly market. The crossroads between the Lamb Inn and the Angel Inn is still called The Square, and if it is imagined without the cluster of buildings round the present Post Office stores, the cottages on the north side of Salisbury Road, Steeple Close and the grassed area in front of the Lamb a considerable space emerges that was almost certainly the fair's site. A market cross was erected on its north side. (An 1804 watercolour by John Buckler (1770-1851) shows the surviving base just below the former chapel, which was on the site of the present church. Hindon folk legend has it that the base still lies beneath the street pavement, but it seems more likely that it was removed when the new church and churchyard wall was built in 1870-1). The fair was granted to take place at Michaelmas, 29th September, a common time for fairs, being a normal date for completion of the harvest.[1]

The fair must have been successful, for 113 years later Edward III granted a new charter for two annual three-day fairs:

> Given at Westminster, January 20th, 1332. Grant, of special grace, to John bishop of Winchester, and his successors, of two yearly fairs at their manor of Hynedon, co. Wilts, one on the vigil, the feast and the morrow of St. Luke, and the other on the vigil, the feast and the morrow of the Ascension.[2]

John Stratford was Winchester's bishop 1323-33, and later elevated to Canterbury. Ascension is movable between 30th April and 3rd June. St. Luke's day is 18th October. The significance of saints' days in relation to fairs will be considered when Hindon's church is featured. Over the centuries the dates of the fair were adjusted. By the 1790s there were two one-day fairs, on the Monday before Whitsun and 29th October (replacing 18th October after the calendar reform in 1752).[3] In the late 19th century this altered to 27th May and 29th October.[4] The fair outlasted the market, which had died by 1889.[5] A single fair on 29th October is listed in *Kelly's Directory* for 1915. It would be surprising if a fair was held in the second year of the First World War (WWI), and the copy for this volume must have been made up in 1914. By the 1920 edition the fair no longer appears. The late Basil Bevis said in 1998 that at the end of the 19th century the fairs were organised by one Cornelius Lamb, who carried a stamp of office. The traders with their carts would assemble at the top of the High Street and, at a signal from Lamb, would hurry down the street to take up their favourite pitches on the pavements. By this time the Square must no longer have been an open space.

The demise of the market can be explained by the development of village shops in this period, but a life of 695 years for the fair requires some explanation.

John Aubrey in the 17th century famously characterized the geology of Wiltshire as being divided into 'chalk and cheese', chalk

being the sheep rearing areas of the Marlborough Downs and
Salisbury Plain, and cheese describing the regions of mixed farming,
mainly in the north of the county. (The phrase is older than Aubrey,
and is of course now a common metaphor for incompatibles). It was
natural that fairs (and markets) would be viable on the divide
between the two ecologies. Add to that Hindon's position near old
communication routes (many of which later became stock
droveways) and things begin to fall into place. Hindon is the last
village on the chalk in this area; two miles to the SW East Knoyle lies
on upper greensand and gault, definitely cheese. On the SW edge of
Salisbury Plain were a number of other market and fair sites such as
Upavon, Market Lavington, Westbury, Warminster, Heytesbury,
Maiden Bradley, Mere, Shaftesbury, and, on the SE edge of the
Dorset chalk, Dorchester. There were many fairs elsewhere, and not
all those just noted were as successful or long surviving as Hindon's
and Warminster's; the concentration on this divide is still striking.

There are few surviving records of trading at Hindon's fair, but
the 1794 reference[3] mentions dealing in cattle and cheese. In 1831
the fair handled cattle, sheep, horses, swine and cheese.[6] Sheep from
the Plain, cattle from Somerset, and cheese from 'cheese'. There
must have been hundreds of small producers to the west that over
time coalesced into the great cheddars of Somerset and vinneys of
Dorset. Cheese, like bacon from the swine, was the handiest food for
wayfarers as well as townspeople, and the demand for it was
considerable. The Winchester bishops' estates at Knoyle and
Downton produced cheese, and in 1805 farmer Wigmore of Knoyle
sent cheese to the annual Winchester cheese fair.[7]

As to horses, they were to become in the 18th century a
dominant feature in Hindon's economy, but there are no records of
them in earlier times. There are indications that in early Tudor years
there was nationally the same divide between horse breeding in
pastoral and mixed farming areas, with brood mares and fillies bred
on the pastoral, and horses, colts and geldings on the mixed.[8] This

later broke down with the increase in private dealing, and there seems to be no evidence that it applied here.

There were also a number of hilltop fairs in Wiltshire, often in isolated positions, often near old communication systems and often associated with prehistoric archaeological features, that many believe to have had very ancient pre-Christian origins.[9] Such was Tan Hill, near Pewsey, which survived well into the 20th century. Such was that held at Yarnbury Castle, a small Iron Age earthwork on the north slope of the Wylye valley and visible from the A303. It was described by W. H. Hudson in *A Shepherd's Life* in 1909. The middle of the earthwork hosted an annual sheep fair from at latest the 18th century until 1916. Sheep pens have left rectangular ridge traces on the eastern side of the central enclosure.

The nearest to home however, was that held on Cold Berwick Hill, only 1 ½ miles from Hindon's fair site (GR ST 920341). This lay

Plate 5. Hut associated with Berwick Hill fair [from a 19th-century watercolour owned by the late Basil Bevis]

within the ecclesiastical parish of Berwick St. Leonard, and was held on 6th November, the feast of St. Leonard. First recorded in the 13th century, its position suggests far earlier origins. A major sheep fair, in the 19th century it traded sheep and horses, and Irish horse dealers proliferated. Bonfires were lit to guide drovers to it, and Hindon publicans brought cartloads of beer to refresh the participants.[10] There were some permanent buildings. In 1833, when the railways were just beginning to threaten the droving trade, the fair penned 14,000 sheep.[11] Thereafter trade declined, and Kelly's dropped the fair from its notice in 1867. However, Ralph Whitlock in his *Wiltshire Folklore and Legends,* 1992, records that the hilltop fairs at Westbury Hill, Yarnbury and Cold Berwick Hill were still held right up to the start of WWI. Basil Bevis had an old watercolour of a hut associated with the Berwick fair, which is reproduced in Pl.5. The Berwick St. Leonard enclosure map of 1840 shows two small structures on the site.[12]

Hundred and Manor

Hundreds, as subdivisions of shires, probably emerged in the 10th century as units for the purposes of taxation, keeping of the peace and settlement of minor local pleas. They seem to have begun as combinations of manors/parishes, and were the remote ancestors of our local government and Justices of the Peace (JP) organisation. Some of their functions straggled on into modern times, long after government-supervised local administration began to take over their main roles.

Wiltshire was originally divided into about 40 hundreds, but through the centuries they were subjected to almost as many reorganisations as local government has suffered in modern times. In 1086 East Knoyle was part of Mere Hundred, and that must have included the part of it that later formed Hindon.[1] In the 13th century the bishops of Winchester, who exercised hundredal power over their scattered estates in Wiltshire, grouped, for administrative purposes, Bishop's Knoyle, Hindon, Fonthill Bishop (which the see had owned since 900) and Bishopstone with Downton Hundred.[2] Hindon and Knoyle remained there until the 19th century, although a Parliamentary survey of the church in Wiltshire in 1649-50, just after Charles I's execution, lists them under Chalke Hundred.[3] This is unexplained.

When East Knoyle was put into Downton Hundred several powers of jurisdiction were retained locally. The bishops' authority in the 10 bailiwicks into which their lands were divided was exercised by a steward, who conducted a biannual *tourn* (session) around Hocktide (2nd Monday and Tuesday after Easter) and Martinmas (11th November). The bailiff of Hindon, the bishops' non-resident representative in the town, presented to this *tourn* when it sat at East Knoyle, as did representatives of the tithings of Fonthill Bishop and Milton.[4] A jury of 12 freemen affirmed on oath their knowledge of, for example, ownership of property. The same bailiff acted as the returning officer when Hindon began to elect members of parliament in 1448.

Records exist of some examples of the way these powers were exercised. In 1464 there were 2 brewers, 9 taverners, 2 innkeepers, 3 bakers and a butcher *amerced* (fined) for breach of food and drink regulations. In the late 15th and the 16th centuries unlawful gaming and moral offences sometimes featured, and about the time of Hindon's Great fire of 1754 the dangerous condition of chimneys and the state of the stocks, blindhouse (lock-up), pillory and market cross were reported.[5]

In the 14th century a tendency began for the chief landholders in Wiltshire to step back from cultivating their estates directly and to lease them or parts of them to others to manage, while remaining as overlords. What began as small freeholds were often added to and merged. In this century the Mossel or Mussel family from small beginnings put together a sizeable estate in Hindon. Two entries in a register of transfers of land that probably pre-date 1300 stipulate that Walter Mossel should pay rent, in one case six silver pennies annually on 'the feast of St. Michael Archangel.'[6] We shall return to the significance of this date later.

In the next century Thomas Tropenell (*c.*1405-88), a lawyer, borough MP, fiercely aspiring Wiltshire squire and client of the Hungerford family, acquired a mortgage to what he called the Manor of Hindon.[7] There was never a manor house here, and no manorial court; no manorial rolls exist. It may be that by calling it such he was boosting his own status, as he seems to have done in

Maiden Bradley, where he also acquired limited land. He was libelled as a 'Perillous, Covetous Man' by others who contested his claim to land in Hindon. He had similar difficulty establishing his claim to Great Chalfield, near Corsham, where he eventually built the beautiful manor house that still stands.

Tropenell acquired lands in East Knoyle, Milton, and Tollard Royal, together with 19 dwellings, a dovecote, a bull and 700 sheep. Whether the Mussels or he lived in Hindon is doubtful, and it seems that none of the owners of substantial land in Hindon from Tropenell's time until the early 20th century were ever resident.[8] The bishops of Winchester remained the landholders in chief until the manor was confiscated by Parliament after the Civil War in 1646.

In Tropenell's time it seems that some fields outside Hindon borough were cultivated in the usual medieval three-field system of strip cultivation, last recorded in 1431. There was also common grazing on Hocken (now Hawking) Down, to the north of the town. All this had probably been enclosed into private ownership by the 16th century, and no trace of strip cultivation seems to survive.[9]

Chapel

When the bishops of Winchester, as lords of the manor of East Knoyle, founded Hindon they provided, in the tradition of Saxon pioneering churches, a chapel for the new inhabitants. The account rolls of the bishopric for 1223-4 record:

> In the building of the chapel of Hindon on the order of the bishop, 13 shillings and 4 pence.[1]

That was a mark. It may be that more money came from another source, but this sum suggests a fairly modest structure.

It is important to realize that although East Knoyle and Hindon within it belonged to the feudal demesne of the bishops of Winchester, they had been within the ecclesiastical jurisdiction of Salisbury diocese since the 11th century. Although Winchester built the chapel, it seems to have provided no endowment for it or for its priest, and the rector of East Knoyle became responsible. This does not seem to have exercised him unduly, and in the late 14th century the chapel appears to have closed.[2] Whether this was due to Knoylian neglect or the Black Death, which struck this part of the country in 1349, is not clear. Knoyle is said to have suffered severely, but its list of rectors appears to show no new appointments at this time. For Hindon there is no record, but the poorer clergy of Wiltshire were severely culled, presumably from dutifully attending the dying, and if a priest and half the inhabitants were dead, it is difficult to see how services here could have been carried on.

(Visitations of plague recurred for centuries and that of 1665 – Pepys' Great Plague of London – also hit here. East Knoyle folk memory talks of a long-gone 'plague stone' past Sheephouse Farm on the Knoyle to Hindon lane at about GR ST 901320, very close to the bowl barrow already mentioned. This would have been a large hollowed-out stone where money, perhaps soaked in vinegar, could be left in exchange for fresh food from an uninfected village. This cannot be confirmed, and it is unclear which village is supposed to have been infected.)

A bishop's register for 1393 lists, for the first time, a 'chaplain of Hindon', Willielmus Stok, so church activity must have recommenced locally by then.[3] The chapel, refounded and probably partly rebuilt (in common with many derelict Wiltshire churches and churchyards at this time), reopened as a 'chapel-of-ease' to East Knoyle parish church (enabling Hindonians to gain ease by not having to attend services two miles away). The chaplain was appointed by Knoyle's rector. It was customary for a rector to keep some control over a chapel-of-ease by retaining the right of, usually, burial in his own churchyard. In Hindon's case it was marriages that its chaplain could not conduct (although, for reasons obscure, a few were registered between 1608 and 1651). Some writers have suggested that this restriction was a source of resentment to Hindon people. This seems unlikely. The principles attending chapels-of-ease were well recognised at the time, and it is surely merrier to walk hand-in-hand with your beloved over the down to Knoyle to be wed than to be carried there on a donkey cart to be buried.

The papal licence that granted the rector of Knoyle appointment of the chaplain of Hindon stipulated that, if he failed to appoint, the inhabitants of Hindon should do so. In the 15th century they endowed the chapel with buildings and land to produce a revenue, and in return received sole right of appointment. The rector, however, continued to receive the tithes of the chapelry,[2] an arrangement that pointed the contrast between East Knoyle, a fairly wealthy living, and Hindon, whose chaplains (sometimes referred to as curates), seem to have lived near the poverty line.

The remainder of the 15th and early 16th centuries have left no records that reveal the condition of Hindon's chapel or its congregation. The Reformation was another matter. Henry VIII assumed headship of the new Church of England in 1534. The monasteries were dissolved between 1536 and 1540. Henry died in 1547 before his plans to extend the dissolution to chantry chapels (private chapels within churches endowed to have masses said for the souls of the worthy departed) could take effect. The nine-year-old Edward VI succeeded. His mentor, Protector Somerset (Edward Seymour, *c*.1500-1552, a major Wiltshire landowner) gave orders for the destruction of all shrines, and an act was pushed through Parliament to confiscate the assets of all chantries, guilds, 'free chapels' and university and other colleges.

Hindon's was listed as a free chapel. The term seems in this case to refer to Hindon's freedom from Knoyle's right to appoint its priest, but other interpretations have been put upon the term elsewhere. The lands supporting the chapel and chaplain were confiscated, leaving them presumably without support. In 1549 the Crown sold part of them to a Laurence Hyde of London (we shall meet other Hydes later), namely 'pasture for 4 oxen yearly in Symerlees (Summerleaze today) in tenure of William Deire and lately belonging to late chapel of Hindon'.[4]

In 1553 royal commissioners trawled the country removing silver from a great number of vestries, often only leaving the minimum plate necessary to maintain services, a blatant raid to replenish a depleted Exchequer. In Hindon 2½ ounces of silver were taken, but a 9 ounce silver chalice was left.[5] It is no longer here, and what later happened to it is, unsurprisingly, not recorded.

Edward VI died in July 1553 and was shortly succeeded by the Catholic Mary Tudor, who did her best to put the clock back as regards church ritual and confiscation of church property.

Fortunately most of Hindon's assets hadn't been sold on. The burgesses petitioned the Crown at some length, complaining about the difficulties in getting to Sunday worship in Knoyle,

> which is distant two miles and more from Hindon and the road between the two so impeded in winter with waters and streams which grow to such depth and breadth that the inhabitants of the borough and their families are unable to cross them almost throughout the whole season.

The burgesses pleaded that they were

> on account of their poverty . . . unable to continue the charges of the chapel and the stipend of the chaplain at their own cost.

This worked, and in October 1558 a royal grant established a chapel in perpetuity 'to celebrate divine service in the said chapel and administer the sacraments from time to time', the living to be called 'the free chapel of Hindon in the parish of Est Knoyle'. It established a corporation of eight governors, complete with seal (not preserved), to hold and manage these assets for the chaplain and chapel, these grants 'without fine or fee'.[6]

This use of the phrase 'free chapel' rather than 'chapel-of-ease' has led to some confusion. Both phrases apply to Hindon's old chapel. 'Chapel-of-ease' is a geographical term for a chapel some distance from its mother parish church. 'Free chapel' denotes its ecclesiastical status. Use of this latter term has caused a number of people to assume that a new (Tudor) church was put up at this point. It is firmly asserted in Sheard's *The History of Hindon*, is printed on several early postcards and features in newspapers and trade directories going back to the 19th century. It may have originated in a misreading of Colt Hoare, who described the surviving medieval chapel in 1822.[7] The fact is that hardly any new parish churches were built in the Tudor period, and Hindon's was not one of them.

Mary died a month after the grant to Hindon chapel. Protestantism was restored under her successor Elizabeth I. We do not know how the twists and turns of this turbulent period affected Hindon's worshippers; there are no records. The general impression in Wiltshire is that the country people kept their heads down; were Protestants under Henry and Edward, Catholics under Mary, and Protestants again under Elizabeth.

One who kept his head up too much was John Story (c.1510–1571), an Oxford civil lawyer. He recanted his Romish opinions in the early months of Edward VI's reign, and sat for Hindon in the parliament of 1547-8. Unable to stomach the reformist legislation under discussion he at one point exclaimed 'Woe unto the land whose king is a child!', for which the Commons clapped him in the Tower, alleged to be the first time it had punished a member for misconduct. He submitted, was released and retired to the Spanish Netherlands. He returned on Mary's accession and, as chancellor of London and Oxford dioceses, bitterly persecuted and burnt protestant heretics. At Elizabeth's accession he took the oath and became MP for Downton, 1558-9. Unwilling to abandon his convictions and unable to control his mouth, he again had to flee to Flanders and resumed persecution of protestants there. Kidnapped by English government agents, he was accused of treason with the Spanish Duke of Alva and grotesquely executed at Tyburn.[8]

To Hindon, Story was an outsider, like most of its MPs, and his experience would not have affected it much. Nor would laws passed from Elizabeth's time onward preventing Catholics from sitting for parliament, holding any public office, upholding the pope's authority, or celebrating Mass, at least openly. The laws against recusancy (absence from the services and sacraments of the Church of England) did, and a succession of acts increased the penalties involved.

In this period Catholics were regarded as a subversive threat, but as time and a half went by, as the wealth and confidence of England increased and the influence of Spain waned, suspicion against them diminished, and laws against recusancy were more laxly applied. This was as well for the Catholics in south west Wiltshire, which was an important focus for them, centred on two families, the Arundells of Wardour and the Stourtons of Stourton. By the 18th century magistrates tended to ignore Catholic services discreetly held on their estates. Hindon contributed a few to the congregation at Wardour. Sources are sparse and sometimes contradictory, but it seems that Hindon Catholics were always in single figures between 1661 and 1783, with a top count of seven in four of those years. They included a glover, a baker, a brazier and a 'barber chyrurgion', Robert White in the late 17th century, and another surgeon, Henry Lambert in the 18th. Philip Kelloway, innkeeper, made numerous appearances at Quarter Sessions for recusancy, and was probably fined, but carried on his trade. Lambert lived quietly in Hindon for decades, and was probably still around in 1783, by which time the number of Catholics had fallen to three.[9]

To go back to the beginning, it was noted earlier that the first grant of a fair to Hindon was to take place at Michaelmas, the feast of St. Michael Archangel (29th September). It is tempting to assume that the dedication of Hindon's first chapel was to the same. In the middle ages fairs, with their connotations of festival and holiday, were commonly held on the patron saint's day, and rents and dues were collected at the same time. We saw earlier that rents for land granted to Walter Mossel were to be paid on that day.

By the end of the middle ages there were about 700 churches in England dedicated to the archangel, variously styled St. Michael, St. Michael and All Angels, St. Michael and All Saints, or St. Michael Archangel. As leader of the hosts of heaven that overthrew Satan, Michael was a favourite dedicatee of very early Saxon churches that replaced pagan shrines, and were consequently often on hilltops or rising ground. Hindon's is on rising ground, but unless there is something we do not know, not of that antiquity.[10]

What is curious however, is that an Angel Inn still stands close by on the edge of the old fair site. In the bar there is an indenture of lease dated 1711 (the earliest surviving reference to its name) that stipulated that rents should be paid by the new tenant biannually, one of the due dates being 'the feast of St. Michael Th'archangell'. Should we postulate a very early date for the establishment of a pub here? (A striking parallel exists at Mere, six miles to the west, whose church is still dedicated to the Archangel. Close by is an Angel Lane, an Angel Corner, and was formerly an Angel Inn.)

Whatever the truth of all of this, the subsequent grant of new fairs in 1332 placed them at Ascension and St. Luke's day, 18th October. The chapel must have been dedicated to Luke by then. It certainly was in 1553, when the royal commissioners robbed it of silver.[5]

Parliament to 1600

Hindon, as a borough,[1] should theoretically have qualified for parliamentary representation in the 13th century, but did not. Choice of which boroughs should qualify would be made by the sheriff of Wiltshire as chief representative of the Crown in the county, but who may not at this stage have regarded Hindon as a sufficiently viable community to merit selection. Choice country-wide seems to have been based on the presence of burgage tenements in the relevant constituency, but selection often seems eccentric.

Hindon was summoned to all parliaments between 1378 and 1385, but did not elect. From 1448, in the reign of the Lancastrian Henry VI, things changed. (see Appendix C; the entry for 1399 is not confirmed in VCH/W v, and may be an error by Manley). So far as the patchy records show, the town regularly elected two members thereafter. At this stage of development the main function of the House of Commons was to vote taxes for the king's use and to receive petitions from individuals and institutions, most of which were devolved to the appropriate central courts of law. There was no fixed duration for sessions; parliaments were summoned when the king needed money and often sat for a few weeks or months only.

What sort of men were Wiltshire's early MP's? In the 14th century there is no evidence to suggest that the Wiltshire boroughs were represented by other than local burgesses, but parliamentary records, so long before Hansard, are very sparse, and many of the names are totally obscure to us. By the time that Hindon started electing MPs things were changing, and increasingly the boroughs were represented by court and crown servants, local gentry and lawyers. This reflected the intrusion into the boroughs by the gentry and aristocracy as landholders, a trend we have already noted. The local townsmen were gradually edged out of consideration, and by the early 17th century this class was virtually extinct as MPs. The Hindon list between 1450 and 1600 contains perhaps 39 names. Three are listed in the sources as knight, six as *armiger* (meaning arms-bearer, which could imply knights or squires displaying their masters' coats-of-arms), 12 as 'gent' or 'esq'. There are four lawyers, an archdeacon, two herbal doctors and a London haberdasher.

Increasingly the lists of the two MPs representing the county (as opposed to the boroughs) of Wiltshire contain the aristocratic names of Thynnes, Herberts, Hungerfords and Seymours, and these sometimes spill over into the boroughs. Wiltshire had a disproportionate number of represented boroughs, 15, sending two members each from the mid-15th century to 1832. This was the major part of Wiltshire's total of 34 members in that period. The smaller boroughs were often invaded by relatives of the big names who could not find seats in their own local areas. So a trend early developed whereby Hindon was hardly ever, if at all, represented by anybody living in the town. Later, as we shall see, the Hydes, Howes and Ludlows were locally based, but William Beckford at Fonthill Gifford was probably the nearest-based of all Hindon's MPs, and surely the biggest local benefactor.

While in the middle ages the bishops of Winchester remained the dominant landholders-in-chief in Hindon (as they did in Downton), their non-resident bailiff acted as the town's returning officer. We can take it that its elected members in parliament represented the interests of the diocese, which in effect would have largely meant the interests of the town, which brought profits to the diocese. During the turbulent years of Reformation, things became more complicated, particularly during the interrupted episcopate of Stephen Gardiner (1531-51 and 1553-5). By the accession of James I in 1603 the bishops' patronage of elections in Hindon seems to have evaporated. We enter a different world thereafter.

The same applies to Winchester's landownership. All bishoprics were deprived by Parliament of their lands in 1650, and the trustees of this process sold the East Knoyle estate to Edmund Ludlow (see below). Although it was returned in 1661 after the Restoration, the bishops of Winchester never regained their power and influence here, and they fade from sight as important to Hindon.

17th Century

If the 16th century was filled with religious controversy and reformation, the 17th witnessed the prolonged conflict between king and parliament, culminating in the Civil War (1642-7 and 1648), the execution of Charles I (1649), the replacement of the Stuart kings and the beginnings of a constitutional monarchy.

Hindon played no particular part in this, but its geographical position enabled it to witness some of the to-ings and fro-ings, and some of its parliamentary representatives played a part.

The manor that Thomas Tropenell had so striven to acquire passed through several hands after his death in 1488: in the 16th and 17th centuries two Mompessons, two Toopes, a Hindon innkeeper Edward Perry, who held it about 1641, Thomas Thynne of the Longleat Thynnes, and Sir Matthew Andrews of Mere.[1] None of these were Hindon MPs.

Names of the MPs (listed in Appendix. C) show similar characteristics as in the 16th century: local aristocracy and gentry. The names of Thomas Lambert in 1625 and Miles Fleetwood in 1640 foreshadow the activities of John Lambert and Charles Fleetwood, their more celebrated relatives on the parliamentary side during the Civil War. By 1630 leaders in Wiltshire had almost all been opposed to Charles I, with the exception of the Thynnes of Longleat, the Arundells of Wardour, Robert Hyde in Dinton (father of Edward, later 1st Earl of Clarendon) and some of the Seymours.

At the start of hostilities in 1642 the royalists were not active in Wiltshire, but after the king moved his headquarters to Oxford late in the year, Hopton's forays into the county brought it into the royal orbit. In March 1643 the parliamentary general Waller marched through the county and linked up with Sir Edward Hungerford.[2]

Let us follow the course of the war in this area through the activities of Edmund Ludlow, who was briefly Hindon's MP in 1659 and 1660-1. Born in Maiden Bradley near Warminster in about 1617, he was the son of Sir Henry Ludlow, a populist MP for Wiltshire county in the Long Parliament (1640-1653). A BA of Trinity College Oxford, Edmund was admitted to Inner Temple and practised as a barrister for a time. He later joined the Earl of Essex's bodyguard with a company of a hundred gentlemen, and fought at first Worcester and Edgehill. Appointed captain of a troop of horse in Hungerford's regiment in April 1643, he joined him in the siege of the 60-year-old Blanche, Lady Arundell at Wardour Castle, five miles south of Hindon. On the way there he had marshalled his forces in the Hindon area, though his later memoirs give no details of this. After a short but gallant defence the castle surrendered on 8 May, and Ludlow was appointed its governor. He was in turn besieged by Henry, Baron Arundell, and after a much admired three-month defence, surrendered in March 1644. With most of his troops he was imprisoned at Oxford, to be later released in an exchange of prisoners.

Promoted colonel and sent back into Wiltshire to raise a regiment of horse and subdue the royalists, he was appointed sheriff of the county, and was involved in several actions of varying success. He was elected MP for Wiltshire (not Hindon) in May 1646, and thereafter played a leading role in the politics of the Civil War and Commonwealth. This included two appointments succeeding Oliver Cromwell in charge of the force attempting to subdue Ireland, a contentious but eventually largely successful command. He was the 40th signatory of Charles I's death warrant in January 1649.

There is no room here to follow all details of his career; what needs to be noticed is that he was consistently on the radical republican wing of the parliamentary movement, to the extent of opposing Oliver Cromwell when he began to show signs of taking on arbitrary power. He continued this after Oliver's death in 1658 when his feeble son Richard, 'Tumbledown Dick', was proposed to succeed as Lord Protector, a highly dubious attempt to revert to the hereditary principle. With that gift for a memorable phrase so common among men of that time, Ludlow declared in the Commons:

> I honour his highness as much as any man that sits here. I would have things settled for his honour and safety, but if we take peoples' liberties from them, they will scratch them back again.

He was returned as MP for Hindon in January 1659, and again in April 1660, just before Charles II's restoration. This was a dangerous time for the surviving regicides, and when proceedings began against them Ludlow slipped away to Geneva, where 'I found good beer, which was a great refreshment to me'. In 1662 he moved to Vevey, near Montreux, where with the aid of the local authorities he was able to make security arrangements that evaded hit squads from London until his death in 1692, aged about 75. (Pl. 6)

Plate 6. Edmund Ludlow [from a drawing by R. White, 1689]

Variously described as 'an honest, dull man', 'wooden headed' and lacking in understanding, he was nevertheless a steadfast republican who never shifted, as so many did, from his wish that 'the nation might be governed by its own consent'.[3]

Ludlow had bought the manor of East Knoyle in 1650, where he continued the old manorial court proceedings.[4] He seems to have been a conscientious member for Hindon in his short representation. When standing in 1660 he expressed his intention of raising the chaplain's salary from £30 to £100; he probably did not have the time to do this. In the election of 1660 he was unsuccessfully opposed by 'Sir Thomas Thinn' (Appdx. C) who :

> ... packed a party (generally consisting of the scum and poore of the parrish, whom he had bribed by giving mony to, and promising more, filling them with drink...), would have the bailiffe to have gone forthwith to the election ... But the bailiff, understanding the duty of his place, refused so to doe. . .[5]

Shades of the 18th century, forsooth! However Thynne got his seat after Ludlow's flight to Switzerland.

On 6 October 1651 the 21-year-old Charles Stuart, crowned King of Scotland but not of England, during his wanderings after defeat at second Worcester, travelled incognito with a few friends via Wincanton, Mere (where they refreshed themselves at the George), Hindon, Chilmark, Teffont and Wilton on their way to Heale House in the Avon Valley, where they stayed a few days.[6] The so-called Monarch's Way on OS Landranger and Explorer maps purports to follow part of this route through Hindon.

At the return of Charles II in 1660 the Hydes were the most significant family in Wiltshire.[2] Originally from Cheshire, they had long been established in these parts – we met a Laurence from London in 1549, above. Edward Hyde, also referred to earlier, was born in Dinton, seven miles to the east of Hindon, in 1609 and became Charles II's Lord Chancellor in exile in 1658. After the

Restoration he led the king's administration until 1667 when, fearful of impeachment, he exiled himself to France and finished writing his *History of the Great Rebellion*. His daughter Anne married James, Duke of York, later James II, under Anglican rites. Their elder daughter Mary married William of Orange and later became his queen. The younger daughter later became Queen Anne. A probably apocryphal story has it that Edward Hyde had married a pot-girl, which led one wit to say:

> It is evident that if Queens of England may have a barmaid for grandmother, lesser mortals need not fret on the subject of ancestry.[7]

The relevance of Edward Hyde to Hindon is that in 1660 he was created Baron Hyde of Hindon, and in 1661 Viscount Cornbury and Earl of Clarendon. Although these titles became extinct in the 18th century, they were recreated in 1756 and 1776 and survive today. The 7th Earl of Clarendon by the second creation and Baron Hyde of Hindon is George Frederick Laurence Hyde Villiers, who lives in Hampshire.[7]

In June 1685 James Scott, 1st Duke of Monmouth, illegitimate son of Charles II and Protestant opponent of the now overtly Catholic James II, raised his banner in revolt at Lyme Regis. The revolt had some initial success, gathering nearly 4000 recruits and capturing Taunton.

Sir Arthur Conan Doyle, in his novel *Micah Clarke*, recounts how Clarke, son of a Cromwellian Ironside, travels from Havant to join Monmouth at Taunton. Making his way north with a rather unlikely collection of eccentrics and misfits, they pass Salisbury and skirt the southern edge of Salisbury Plain below the skyline in order to evade patrols of the king's horse. Passing by Fovant they see Hindon in the distance:

> Methinks I see one straight line of houses there . . . but it is distant and the shimmer of the sun disturbs my sight . . . It must be the hamlet of Hindon . . .

Hamlet! This is an otherwise vivid description that suggests that Conan Doyle had walked the course, although he may have placed the viewpoint of the companions wrongly. What is more interesting is that he got the dangers of travelling up the Nadder Valley right. In 1685 four men were arrested in Hindon on suspicion of going to join Monmouth. Two were 'factious and seditious persons against the King and government'. One was suspected of having run from his colours. Two had landed at Lyme as officers' servants and run from Bridgwater.[8] Did Conan Doyle know this?

The rising had no chance and was crushed at Sedgemoor on 5 July. Three years later an altogether more formidable enterprise was mounted that enabled Hindon to witness a turning point in English history.

At the not-so-secret invitation of a number of English political heavyweights who had become increasingly disturbed at James II's attempts to re-establish Catholicism, William of Orange landed at Torbay on 5 November 1688 with an army of 11,000 foot and 4,000 horse, a *mélange* of British regiments from the Netherlands, Dutch, Swedes, Germans and Swiss. Waiting for support to come in, he proceeded by slow stages to Crewkerne and reached Hindon, his first stop in Wiltshire, on 3 December. One has to imagine the officers of this force quartered in Hindon houses and the men encamped in the fields around.

William was dined that day by the widow of Edward Hyde of Hatch at Berwick House in Berwick St. Leonard, a mile to the east along the Salisbury road. Present was Henry Hyde, 2nd Earl of Clarendon (1638–1709), (son of Edward the first Earl), who had been appalled by his own son Edward's earlier defection to William. He nevertheless took it upon himself, as shire representative, to welcome William. Also present was John Churchill, later the great 1st Duke of Marlborough, who had been created Baron Churchill in 1685 and, only on 7 November 1688, promoted Lieutenant-General in James II's horse guards.

Any fears that conflict with James' larger forces, that had lain at Salisbury, would ensue evaporated when the king, abandoning his responsibilities, withdrew from the city and later slipped away to France. William was welcomed into Salisbury on 4 December, colours flying, drums beating, church bells pealing.[9]

Berwick House where this crucial meeting took place was owned by the Grobham Howes (Appdx. C). Their relative Sir Scrope Howe, 1st Viscount Howe, had earlier declared for William at Nottingham. He was the grandfather of Richard, Earl Howe, victor of the sea battle against the French dubbed the 'Glorious First of June', in 1794.[10] The 17th century house no longer stands. About 1900 it was ruinous, and removed to Ashley Wood nearby to form the nucleus of a new house by Detmar Blow, later also pulled down.[11]

Parliament – 1700-1832

Sir Matthew Andrews, who held the manor of Hindon at the end of the 17th century, sold it to Thomas Jervois in 1701.[1] Jervois was Hindon's MP in 1702 (Appdx. C.). So was Reynolds Calthorpe of Elvetham in Hampshire in 1698, 1705, 1708, 1713 and 1714. He owned the Angel Inn in 1711.[2] In about 1738 Henry Calthorpe, a relative, bought the Hindon estate from Jervois. He later became Sir Henry Calthorpe, 1st Baron Calthorpe of Elvetham after representing Bramber as MP from 1774-1790.[3] Owning Hindon manor enabled the holder to appoint candidates to stand for election in his interest.

By the time of Monmouth's rebellion in 1685 it is possible to discern a division into parliamentary groupings that began to be dubbed Whig and Tory. These were originally terms of abuse derived from descriptions of different sorts of Scottish and Irish bandits. The Whigs, whom we would describe as on the left, wanted parliamentary limitation of the crown's powers combined with religious toleration, but only for protestants. The Tories were the church and king party, supporters of hereditary succession, who had only joined with the Whigs to oust James II when his Catholic aspirations became too blatant.

After a period of Tory dominance under Anne (reigned 1702-14), the Whigs had it all their own way until the accession of George III in 1760, and to an extent beyond. As a broad generalisation it can be said that the 18th-century borough seats, often corrupt, tended to be Whig whereas the county seats, dominated by landed families and often amply filled by squires and parsons, were more Tory. We have seen that in the previous century Hindon's MPs were exemplified by Edmund Ludlow, on the extreme republican side of the parliamentary movement. The leftish tendency continued, and Hindon was nearly always Whig. It was a period of constituency management that was controlled by Whig party chiefs and resulted in their domination of what became known as rotten boroughs.

Hindon should probably technically be described as a burgage borough. Voting qualification went to those paying *scot and lot*, a form of parish rates, *scot* going to the poor, *lot* for church maintenance. This worked out at 113 voters in 1735,[4] about 200 in 1754,[5] and 210 in 1774.[6] This was large enough to be worth bribing, and small enough to do so with no vast expenditure. But whereas in the county seats local landowners could easily influence selection and voting, the boroughs represented wider interests, and merchants, lawyers, government officials and adventurers often sat. Not all the occupations of Hindon MPs in this period are known, but there were at least seven lawyers, a soldier, two ex-East India Company employees, two writers, three West Indian planters, a travelling archaeologist and a Salisbury clothier. These would mostly have stood in the interests of the landowners, Calthorpe and Beckford (of whom more later), or other senior Whigs, but there were sometimes enough candidates to cause the occasional upset. James Dawkins the archaeologist (elected 1754) was a Jacobite supporter and financier, a very un-Whiggish thing to be, and Benjamin Hobhouse, before he stood for Hindon in 1806, had served as Secretary of the Board of Control under Henry Addington, 1st Viscount Sidmouth, PM 1801-4, who was not much of a Whig party man and had certain Tory characteristics. He was MP for Devizes from 1783 to 1805, and paid for the Market Cross, still in the town.

As so many of these men were not local people but ambitious for office and able to afford to look for a berth here, there is not much point in detailing their careers, which are not relevant to the town. It might just be noted that William Blackstone (elected 1761) later knighted, was a judge and author of the famous *Commentaries on the Laws of England*. It is also worth mentioning Henry Fox (elected 1734), father of the more famous and wittier Charles James Fox. An archetypal systems Whig, he went on to represent other constituencies, hold various offices and eventually become secretary of state for foreign affairs, about which he knew nothing. He adhered to Thomas Pelham-Holles, Duke of Newcastle (curiously both of upon-Tyne and under-Lyme). Personally incorruptible, Newcastle became mid-century the great puppet-master of Whig patronage, controlling (fairly incompetently) the secret service fund. This was nothing to do with espionage but a Treasury account wielded solely by the Duke to influence elections and appointments to office. Fox wrote to Newcastle in 1756 complaining that only £313 11s. had been allocated to Hindon for a by-election that year.

> If no help is to be had in a venal borough, venal boroughs must go to your enemies.[7]

What is interesting is that the Calthorpe map of 1748 (Pl. 7) shows that Newcastle owned a small property in Hindon. The significance of this must be left to future researchers to investigate.

Calthorpe's interest in the borough began to be invaded when the elder William Beckford (1709–1770) purchased the estate of Fonthill, two miles to the east, in 1745. He had inherited a sugar estate in Jamaica, worked by slaves, that made him enormously rich. Returning to England he became thrice MP for the City of London, once Sheriff and twice Lord Mayor, which earned him the nickname the Alderman. Originally Tory, he became a radical and outspokenly speechifying Whig, even denouncing slavery, from which he got his money. James Boswell criticized these 'yelps for liberty', but he was not lily-white either, being in favour of the slave trade.[8] Beckford was a crony of William Pitt the elder, the 'Great Commoner', like Ludlow

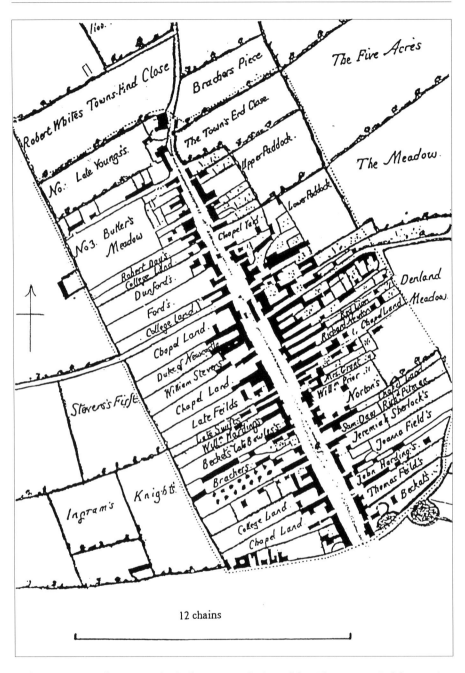

*Plate 7. From the map of Hindon commissioned by Sir Henry Calthorpe in
1748 [redrawn by P. Cawthorne, 2000]*

an alumnus of Trinity, Oxford, PM 1756-61, strategic genius and victor of the Seven Years' War (1756-61), to the financing of which Beckford made substantial loans. The families were to remain in contact.

The Alderman's growing interest in Hindon led to an agreement in 1754 to share influence in the borough with Calthorpe. This proceeded fairly amicably until Beckford died in 1770, leaving his son William, age 9, an heir in Chancery.

With Calthorpe neglecting his own interests, this led to a proliferation of candidates for the infamous general election of 1774. Hindon's chaplain, John Nairn, introduced to the town as 'General Gold' Richard Smith, a former East India Company soldier, who he said was prepared to advance five guineas a head to each elector, with more to come. Nairn, disguised as 'Mr. Punch', enticed votes for Smith at up to ten guineas a throw; some voters signed receipts purporting to issue from a fictitious character called 'Glenbucket'. Another stranger, Thomas Brand Hollis, member of a republican family with a strongly anti-corruption tradition but a very simple fellow, also stood. He was promoted by a Salisbury butcher, John 'Jobber' Stevens, who promised 'to make Hell roar and the Devil dance at Hindon'. Quite how such resonant words could translate into a political programme was not made clear. Against these two stood James Calthorpe, a relative of Sir Henry's and Richard Beckford, the Alderman's illegitimate elder son.

Bribery was gross, and Smith and Brand Hollis were elected. This was too much even for the 18th-century House of Commons, which had a high opinion of its own worth. It voided the election on petition from Calthorpe and Beckford, and recommended that Hindon be disfranchised. This aroused violent opposition from many interested quarters and the proposal was dropped. However a new election was called and Richard Smith and Henry Dawkins, a local landowner were elected. Smith and Brand Hollis were later fined and imprisoned, and Smith's second election was annulled. A period of chaos was only ended when Edward, Baron Thurlow became Lord Chancellor and could so re-order the Beckford interest that the Beckford–Calthorpe equilibrium was restored.[9]

Namier famously classified the rotten boroughs accordingly to their loyalty or otherwise to their candidates: as 'faithful wives', who nevertheless chose partners according to their perceived future prosperity; as 'kept mistresses', expensive, relatively faithful, but, not bound by contract; or 'prostitutes', ready to receive any adventurer for money. He had no difficulty in seeing Hindon at this stage as a fallen woman.[10]

William Beckford, the Alderman's second son (1760–1844) had as godfather William Pitt, created Earl of Chatham in 1766, and Thurlow as guardian. Chatham had been bequeathed a home at

Plate 8. William Beckford jnr

Burton Pynsent, near Langport in Somerset, where he lived in retirement for a while until the old hypochondriac decided that the Levels were bad for his health, and returned to Surrey. Beckford's mother had allowed her son William to stay there occasionally, where he is said to have got on with Chatham's own son William, a year younger. Later in life they were not so compatible; one might say they were chalk and cheese. We shall meet the younger Pitt later, on the road.

There is no room in this account to tell the story of the extraordinary younger Beckford, traveller, Grand Tourist, self-exile, author, connoisseur, collector of books and art, composer of sorts, builder, eccentric, reclusive, bisexual. The tale is pretty well known locally, and here we can only consider his relationship with Hindon as landowner, MP and benefactor. (Pl. 8)

He was not a natural politician, and when he came of age did not want to turn a sitting member out of the Hindon seat. However he clearly wanted to enter parliament in order to graduate to a peerage, as he confided to Thurlow. He sat for Wells, 1784-90, 'but found the experience distasteful'. The Courtenay scandal of 1784 finished his chances of ennoblement, and he fled abroad. In 1790 he returned himself for the Hindon seat, but again spent most of his time abroad, and when summoned to return for the recall of the House in 1794 applied for the Chiltern Hundreds.

Before this, and at the start of the French Revolution, he had been in Paris, and perhaps witnessed the execution of Louis XVI. He seems to have shared some of the innocent excitement of some Englishmen at this apparent demonstration of the principles of liberty, such as Charles James Fox, Coleridge and Wordsworth, who wrote:

> Bliss was it in that dawn to be alive,
> But to be young was very heaven.

In this republican mode Beckford was following the tradition of Ludlow and others, but as a British MP his behaviour was extraordinary. His latest biographer describes him at this time as a 'play-acting Jacobin'. During the short-lived Peace of Amiens (1802-3) that temporarily halted the long war with France, he was again in Paris, and apparently lost in admiration of Napoleon. Resentful of the British ruling class that had ostracised him, he seems to have felt that he should keep in with the French in case a successful invasion might work to his advantage. Treason? For an impractical fantasist, perhaps not.[11]

From 1806 to 1820 Beckford was again Hindon's MP, but seems not have sat too much, and described himself as 'a perfect stranger to all parliamentary forms and ceremonies'. He did attend the Regent's opening of Parliament in 1812, and again in 1817, but, for his own financial relief, was usually abroad during sessions. Riddled by debt he made an arrangement that enabled him to relinquish the seat in 1820.[12]

He seems never to have been entirely sure why he wanted to be elected, or even sure of election, but spent considerably to be voted in. We have his election expenses for 1812, a huge total of £2,641 paid out for administrative costs, agency fees, secret service money (£100), transport, tips, dinners and booze, and other obscure charges. A total of £474 on tabs at seven surviving inns.[13] Not surprising that at one election a 'free' elector, well oiled, is said to have declared:

> If Squire had sent his great dog we should have chosen him, all one as if it were you, Sir.

The first of the great 19th-century Reform Bills, that disfranchised Hindon, passed into law on 4 June 1832. It followed months of parliamentary confusion, localised rioting in the countryside in protest at agricultural conditions, and a widespread public feeling that aristocratic control of representation must go. Wiltshire seats were reduced from 34 to 18, the county vote being split between north and south areas, with two seats each. Nine MPs in Wiltshire voted for their own disfranchisement, including E. J. Stanley, one of the two Hindon members. Any Hindonians who were qualified to vote under the new rules would thereafter have to vote in the South Wiltshire constituency. Their number is not known.[14]

Transport and Travellers

If Hindon's prosperity or otherwise always depended on its geographical position, then the vast increase in travel in the late 17th and 18th centuries determined the town's economic success in the latter. Before that, most people travelled on horseback or on foot, which did little damage to the medieval roads and old trackways. It was the later increase in wheeled traffic, however, that destroyed many routes.

Before that happened droving, the movement of meat on hoof and trotter, had long sustained the markets and especially fairs of medieval England. In the middle ages, as towns grew too large to produce their own meat, droving along lanes and trackways increased. Hindon was no exception. As London expanded by ten times the rate of the rest of the country in the late 16th and early 17th centuries, cattle was driven in quantity from the Somerset Levels and south Wales direct to Smithfield Market. Much of this passed along what we know as the Ox Drove, about a mile to the north of Hindon. Sheep were also driven in huge quantities to local and distant fairs. The wide verges of at least five of the eight present roads radiating from Hindon suggest that they carried sheep, mainly from Dorset and Salisbury Plain, to Hindon market and fair, and to Berwick fair and beyond. Some of these routes and fairs are shown in Plate 9.

No doubt some drovers were unlicensed rogues, but from the reign of Elizabeth I they were officially regulated by statute. They

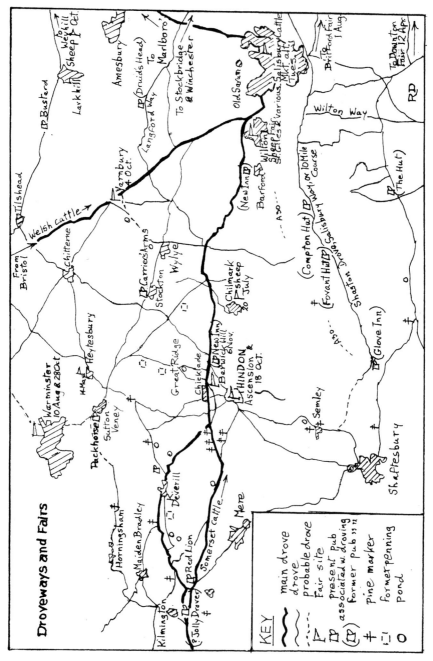

Plate 9. Droveways and fairs [author]

had to be over 30 and married householders; their licenses were renewed annually. They had an honourable status, travelled armed, carrying money and messages, and in due course were almost travelling bankers, carrying promissory notes and bills of exchange that could be exchanged at big fairs.[1] In Hindon they may have used the building in the High Street still called Bank House.

As the drovers wound their often vast herds and flocks through the countryside, they would hire pasture for the night from innkeepers known to them; in some areas, such as the Yorkshire Dales, many inns catered specifically for them. Here there are remains of several pens on the slope up to the Great Ridge, and it is likely that the former New Inn at Chicklade Bottom catered for the trade.[1] Some of the hilltop routes of these droves are marked by deliberate 18th century planting of Scots pines, to guide drovers up to the high routes and pennings.[2] (Pl. 10)

Despite the atrocious deterioration of Britain's roads in the 17th century there was clearly late in that century considerable traffic through Hindon. A government survey of available accommodation and stabling in Wiltshire in 1686, mainly for the purposes of billeting troops, lists, in an adult population of 311, 47 guest beds and stabling for 88 horses (and mentions that there had been 10 innkeepers in 1620).[3] This needs to be borne in mind in connection with William of Orange's armed passage through the town two years later (q.v.).

The first stage coach from London to Devon travelled in 1658, when the London to Exeter run took four days. This time was halved just over a hundred years later. By 1784 the run was done in 32 hours, and by 1832 in 17½ hours at an average speed of 10mph.[4] Hindon became a stage on one of several routes from London to the south west in this area, which ushered in the greatest period of the town's prosperity. It was briefly interrupted by the Great Fire of 1754, considered in the next chapter. But just five years later the Fisherton Turnpike Trust was empowered by Parliament to under-

Plate 10. Scots pine droveroute markers on A303 above Two Mile Down
[photo: author]

take maintenance of the Salisbury–Wilton–Hindon–Willoughby Hedge (GR ST 870337) route west along the Nadder Valley, together with part of the road from Salisbury to Warminster as far as Heytesbury and a ridgeway route across Salisbury Plain to Devizes.[5] Hindon's portion of the road was built by 1762, with toll houses at Wilton, Chilmark and Willoughby Hedge.

Such trusts were a privatisation of road care, depending on subscription by local interests: landowners, traders, merchants, manufacturers and councils; and usually each covered about 30 miles of road. Their purpose was to stimulate trade by the improvement of road surfaces. The initial techniques used predated Thomas Telford's re-making of the Bristol Road in 1784, and John Macadam's later surfacings using stones, flints and granite chippings. (It is worth noting that it was General George Wade, MP for Hindon 1714-15 (see Appendix C) who from 1726 reconstructed roads in the Scottish highlands in the wake of the first Jacobite rebellion, using the techniques of Telford's and Macadam's predecessor John Metcalf).[6]

Fisherton Trust's responsibilities ended at Willoughby Hedge; westwards was the Wincanton Trust's. It seems that the initial turnpiking of this section followed the ancient Harroway/Hardway route into Somerset across Charnage Down to Whitesheet Hill (GR ST 805349), by Long Lane to Alfred's Tower (GR ST 745352), and so very steeply down Kingsettle Hill into Somerset at Brewham.[7] Getting back up this hill must have presented problems to heavier stage coaches and the gentler slope to Mere on the line of the present A303 was surfaced instead. It seems to be so indicated on maps from the 1780s.[8]

The Amesbury Turnpike Trust improved the route from Andover via Wylye and Chicklade to Willoughby Hedge from 1761-5, and this also affected Hindon's economy.

The stage coach system linked the capital with the provinces, boosted trade and enabled the middle classes to get about with a reasonable chance of arriving at their intended destinations according to the timetable forecasts. The system was mainly centred on London. The coaches were built and owned by people who called themselves 'contractors', and who hired them out to 'proprietors' who horsed and manned the vehicles, drew up their timetables and organised innkeepers along the route to lease the horses required for their stages.[9]

Coaches were drawn by four horses, at first travelling the whole route, slowly. Later 20-mile and then 10-mile stages were introduced, with change of horses along the route. With better springing and road improvements times improved rapidly, as did the survival rate of horses. About 1800 the general introduction of front and rear boots gave a safer ride to outside passengers, carried more baggage and enabled more passengers of the 'lower sort' to travel on top.[9] The golden age was from about 1825, when proprietors ran cut-throat competition with their rivals and sent their gaily liveried vehicles to all parts of the nation.

This developed slowly, and in earlier times delays were frequent, particularly when privately owned carriages competed with stage coaches for horses at the various stages. In October 1786 Parson Woodforde recorded in his diary that, returning to Norfolk after visiting relatives in Bruton, Somerset, he travelled

> from Wincaunton . . . onto Meer and there changed Chaises and went on to Hindon – there we were obliged to bait the horses as we could get no Chaise and then went on in the same Chaise for Sarum. NB At the same Inn at Hindon was Mr. Pitt the prime Minister in the same Dilemma as we were all the horses being engaged – he was going to Burton Pynsent.

A different world! Here is the younger Pitt we have already met (PM 1783-1801 and 1804-6), travelling without security and probably only accompanied by a companion or a secretary, and stranded for lack of transport.

Coach travel was not without its hazards. The *Salisbury and Winchester Journal* reported in November 1783 that:

> about 5 o'clock a Stage Coach was overturned in passing the corner of the Lamb Inn, Hindon, by which an outside passenger of Sherborne had his leg broken in two places, and his collar bone put out. Several ladies and inside passengers were also bruised and the Coach received Great Injury.

By 1830 24 stage coaches a week, each drawn by four horses and hoping to carry four well-to-do passengers inside and six to eight noisy rabble on top, stopped at Hindon, probably for change of horses and exchange of packages and passengers. The *North Devon Telegraph* left London on the 'down' route every day except Sunday at 1.30pm, scheduled to reach the Lamb Inn via Andover, Salisbury and Wilton at 3am, before going on to Taunton (arr. 9.30am) and Barnstaple (arr. 6pm). The *Subscription* left London at 5pm and, stopping only at Basingstoke and Andover, reached the Swan Inn, across the High Street from the Lamb, also at 3am en-route to Honiton and Exeter. These coaches would cross with their 'up' equivalents, the *Telegraph* reaching Hindon at 11pm and the *Subscription*, at 5am. The two inns thus had to handle four coaches six nights a week, and had to be 24-hour operations.[10]

The proprietor of these two services was Edward Sherman, the second biggest operator from London at the time, who worked from the Bull and Mouth Inn, St. Martins-le-Grand.[11] His coaches, spanking smart in primrose yellow and black, clattered through Hindon in the middle of the night, presumably unseen by drooling small boys, who one hopes were all long a-bed.[9]

Later, services were reduced as railways began to encroach on the trade. In 1842 the *North Devon* called at the Swan rather than the Lamb every Monday, Wednesday and Friday at the more civilized hour of 3pm *en route* to Barnstaple, and on the return every Tuesday, Thursday and Saturday at 1pm, *en route* to Southampton where it connected with the railway to London. The *Defiance*, jointly run by Sherman and J. Nelson, called at the Lamb en route from Andover to Exeter at 2am, and on the return to Andover via Salisbury at 2.30am.[12]

The Royal Mail service was a separate system. It replaced the 16th-century organisation of 'postboys' who rode the mail, often idly, on horseback over an intricate network of routes. Hindon housed two of them in 1773.[13]

In the 1780s a new order was established, pushed by the younger Pitt as PM. Special coaches were commissioned, shorter, higher, lighter and faster than the lower-slung stage coaches. They carried four paying passengers inside, none on top, and were supervised by a guard carrying a blunderbuss. Again, innkeepers along the route were commissioned to provide horses. They ran seven days a week, demanded precedence on the road, and paid no tolls. By the 1830s, painted scarlet on the lower body and underframe; with black boots, upper panels and roof; with gold piping and royal arms on the door they were kings of the road and reckoned, barring accidents, to time their arrival at stages to the minute. This was probably the most efficient pre-industrial system of mail delivery in history.

In 1837 the *Quicksilver* Royal Mail coaches did not transit Hindon, but travelling by Andover, used the Amesbury Trust's turnpike, dropping mailbags for Hindon at Chicklade (Pl. 11), probably at the New Inn at Chicklade Bottom already mentioned. On to Exeter (16 hours, 34 minutes including halts for meals, changes of horses, and PO business), and so to Devonport and Falmouth, where they connected with the packet boats for West Indies, America, Lisbon, Brazil and the Mediterranean.[14] A restored example of one of these famous coaches is at Plate 12.

Hindon was not only a stage on the coaching routes. In the early 19th century it saw the heavy waggons of several firms, notably those of Thos. Russell & Co., a concern going back to the 17th century, pass between Wincanton and Salisbury. At least between 1816 and 1821 their wagons, like that in Pl. 13 could have been seen here, with teams of eight shire-type horses pulling loads of up to 8 tons in waggons weighing 8 tons, with 5 ft diameter hind wheels carrying 9-inch treads. Travelling at about 2mph, the London to Exeter route took 4½ days. They may have stopped here to put down and pick up packages.

Their main commerce was of west country cloth, especially kerseys and serge, sent to satisfy the demands of a rapidly expanding London; woollen cloth being returned on the 'down' route. Sailcloth, hops, butter, shop goods, seeds and nursery goods were also transported, and so were private customers' heavy baggage and aristocrats' house contents and pictures. Passengers were also taken, and this was the much cheaper and customary way of travelling of the poor.[15]

The long distance routes clearly had to be connected by cross routes and by cart and carriage trade providing local services. Somebody would have had to fetch the mail bags dropped at

Plate 11 (opposite). Timebill for 'Quicksilver' mail coach, London to Devonport, 1837

Contractors' Names.	Number of Passengers.		Stages.	Time Allowed.	Despatched from the General Post Office, the of , 1837, at 8 p.m.
	In.	Out.	M. F.	H. M.	Coach No. {With timepiece sent out {safe, No. to .
					Arrived at the Gloucester Coffee-House at .
			⎰12 2		Hounslow.
Chaplin .			{ 7 1	} 2 47	Staines.
			⎱ 9 7		Bagshot. Arrived 10.47 p.m.
			⎰ 9 1		Hartford Bridge.
Company.			{10 1	} 2 54	Basingstoke.
			{ 8 0		Overton.
			⎱ 3 5		Whitchurch. Arrived 1.41 a.m.
Broad . .			{ 6 7	0 39	Andover. Arrived 2.20 a.m.
			⎱13 7	1 19	Amesbury. Arrived 3.39 a.m.
Ward . .			9 5	0 55	Deptford Inn. Arrived 4.34 a.m.
Davis . .			{ 0 5	} 0 41	Wiley.
			{ 6 5		Chicklade. Arrived 5.15 a.m.
					(Bags dropped for Hindon, 1
			⎰ 6 6		Mere. [mile distant.)
			{ 7 0		Wincanton.
Whitmash			{13 4	} 2 59	Ilchester.
			⎱ 4 1		Cart Gate. Arrived 8.14 a.m.
			⎰ 2 6		Water Gore, 6 miles from South
Jeffery .			{	} 0 44	Petherton.
			{		Bags dropped for that place.
			⎱ 5 1		Ilminster. Arrived 8.58 a.m.
Soaring .			8 1	} 0 25 / 0 46	Breakfast 25 minutes. Dep. 9.23.
					Yarcombe, Heathfield Arms. Arrived 10.9 a.m.
Wheaton .			8 7	0 51	Honiton. Arrived 11 a.m.
			⎰16 4	1 34	Exeter. Arrived 12.34 p.m.
Cockram .			{	0 10	Ten minutes allowed.
			{10 3	} 1 57	Chudleigh.
			⎱ 9 3		Ashburton. Arrived 2.41 p.m.
			⎰13 2		Ivybridge.
			{ 6 6		Bags dropped at Ridgway for
Elliott . .			{	} 2 33	Plympton, 3 furlongs distant.
			{ 4 0		Plymouth. Arrived at the Post
			⎱ 1 7		Office, Devonport, the : of
					, 1837, at 5.14 p.m. by
					timepiece. At by clo·k.
					Coach No. {Delivered timepiece
			216 1	21 14	arr. . {safe, No. to .

The time of working each stage is to be reckoned from the coach's arrival, and as any lost time is to be recovered in the course of the stage, it is the coachman's duty to be as expeditious as possible, and to report the horse-copers if they are not always ready when the coach arrives, and active in getting it off. The guard is to give his best assistance in changing, whenever his official duties do not prevent it.

By command of the Postmaster-General.

GEORGE LOUIS, *Surveyor and Superintendent.*

Plate 12. Restored 'Quicksilver' Royal Mail coach from the London to Devonport route [Photo: courtesy of Streetlife Museum of Transport, Hull City Museums]

Chicklade in 1837. In the 19th century *Kelly's Directory* lists some of these services. In 1855 Richard Perrott of Hindon carried to Shaftesbury and Salisbury two days a week, and James Everett twice to the Chough Inn at Salisbury. Hibbert of Tisbury called at the Queen's Head in Hindon, linking to Warminster on Thursdays. In 1875 George Snook of Hindon carried to Shaftesbury and Salisbury; Hull of Tisbury called at the Grosvenor Arms in Hindon (named Angel Inn before 1830s and since 2001) en route to Warminster, presumably along the old trackway over Hawking Down, now a no-through road.

It is obvious that the horse was a dominant feature of Hindon's economy, and on market and fair days the place must have been full of the animals. Even so, there is a persistent legend of the 'it is said that . . .' variety, often mechanically reiterated in glossy magazine articles, that the Lamb Inn at one time had stabling for 300 horses (a claim once appropriated by a former landlord of the Grosvenor Arms to apply to his own pub). Anyone familiar with the ground must be sceptical of this, and the figure of 88 for the whole village in the 1686 survey (q.v.) must put it in some perspective.

In 1859 the London and South Western railway to Salisbury was extended through Tisbury to the west as the Salisbury and Yeovil Railway. By-passing Hindon up the gentler incline of the Nadder valley, this was to be the death knell for its coaching trade and also for the old drove roads. Different centres and markets grew up along the new routes, and it was no longer economical to maintain the slow old waggon routes or move meat on the hoof. But this was not the finish of the horse in Hindon. The new railway station in Tisbury used horse-drawn carts to collect and deliver parcels and freight in the villages around until the 1920s. In that

Plate 13. An 18th-century carrier's wagon [Aquatint by J.B. Pyne]

decade Fred White hired out light carriages to local people, particularly to and from Tisbury.[16] Before the 20th century, most brewing in Hindon was done locally, but increasingly the larger breweries like Wadworth in Devizes delivered widely by their splendid horse-drawn drays. Even in the 1950s, local deliveries of milk from Hindon's two dairies were done by horse.[17] This rich history was memorably recalled with a horse cavalcade during Hindon's millennial celebrations in 2000 that also represented many of the events recounted here.

Trade, Crafts and Phoenix, 1700 - 1830

In considering Hindon's economic success in the 18th century, we have first to take notice of its pivotal event, the Great Fire in mid-century.

On a windy day, 2 July 1754, between 2 and 3 in the afternoon, a spark from the forge in the workshop of John Tyler, a cutler, caught the thatch of his cottage, allegedly towards the top end of the High Street on the western side, and turned into a blaze. The *Bath Journal* recorded it thus:

> The wind being pretty high, and the greatest part of the houses thatched, it soon catch'd hold of Mr. Day's Malt-house adjoining; and the Wind shifting, the Flames were driven to the opposite Side of the Street, and burnt down about Eighty Houses; the Wind returning, the fire was removed to the same side and burnt down about sixty more. It did some small damage to the Church [i.e. Chapel]. Most of the Household goods, Moneys, Writings, etc., belonging to the Inhabitants were destroyed by the merciless flames. One person was burnt to Death, and another hurted. Out of the fourteen inns and Public-Houses, there was only one preserved. A vast quantity of beer was lost, as well as Hay, Corn and other Grain; so that the poor Inhabitants are reduced to the greatest Extremity and Want; some having lost their All. The Bucket-Wells being so very deep, and the place in some confusion, no Water could be come

at. And the report of the Buckets being cut off, and carried away by ill-designing People, is entirely false; tho' indeed one was for the sake of the Rope and was done with a design to pull down a House in Order to stop the Progress of the Flames.

Undoubtedly a disaster, it is difficult to gauge from newspaper accounts alone the completeness or otherwise of the destruction. No local fire insurance records exist for this period, and there is no evidence as to how many businesses or families were ruined. Some buildings, like No. 8 in the lower High Street, have scorched timbers in their roof space, but these have been re-used and cannot be proved to relate to the fire (Pl. 14). The map of the town commissioned by its main landowner, Lord Calthorpe six years earlier (Pl. 7) shows a jumble of buildings occupying the presumably once open site of the medieval fair, and a building in the middle of the High Street, perhaps the old shambles. These no longer appear in the Tithe Apportionment map of 1844 (Pl. 15). Six re-cast bells

Plate 14. Scorched roof timber in roof space of No. 8, High Street. A survivor of the fire? [Photo: author]

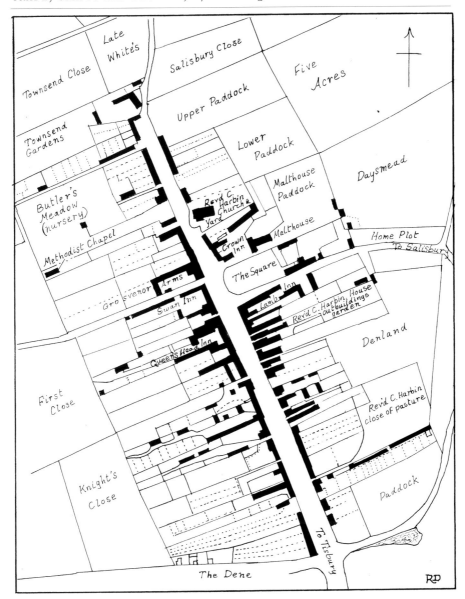

Plate 15. Transcription of part of map attached to schedule of Hindon's rent charge apportionment in lieu of tithe, 1844

were hung in the chapel that year, so damage there could not have been serious. The architecture of the present Lamb Inn suggests that it was built about this time, so it may have been a casualty then. A marriage settlement of 1752 describes the Angel Inn as 'newly erected'.[1] This may be the present building, of rendered brick with tiled roof, which could have survived.

It is said that many were sleeping out in the woods to the south that July. It is clear that the relief resources of the time were deployed to help. The *Bath Journal* reported immediate local donations of money and provisions. Lord Folkestone was reported to have given over £100 (Sir Jacob Bouverie, Bt., former MP for Salisbury, created Viscount Folkestone 1747). In February 1755 a Lord Chancellor's Brief was issued; this authorised an appeal to be published nationally. Few records of it survive, but the parish accounts of St. Nicholas, Ash, near Canterbury record that £1.12s.5½d was collected there.

Recovery was surprisingly rapid, and it must be assumed that Calthorpe, as the owner of most of the buildings, had a good reason to be involved. Hindon was in a period of economic growth, and merchants and innkeepers had every incentive to rebuild, perhaps in a grander style than before. Limestone was used, but some of the smaller properties used brick and tiles from local sources. Land tax assessments (LTAs), which survive for several years in this period, show that payments were almost back to pre-fire levels within two years.[2]

With this background we can look at some of the occupations of Hindonians in this period. The few farmers with smallholdings round about lived in the town rather than outside. Thomas Field was the top land tax payer in 1741, assessed at £1.12s.0d.[2] His house and garden is shown in Pl. 7. But farms were in decline, and although some survived into the 19th century, they were not a significant part of the economy.

Between 1700 and 1750 the following trades were listed in wills and tax assessments: blacksmith, butcher, carpenter, clockmaker, cordwainer, cutler, glover, hatter, innkeeper, maltster, stonemason, surgeon, thatcher. Four shops are mentioned in 1748, but with no indication as to what they sold. From 1750-1800 there are added: auctioneer, bookseller/stationer, cooper, currier, grocer, horse collar maker, mercer, plumber, saddler, siever and tailor. Evidence given to inquiry into the rotten election of 1774 lists: an apothecary, 2 bakers, a blacksmith, 3 breeches makers, a bricklayer, 4 butchers, 5 carpenters, 4 clockmakers, a cooper, 2 cordwainers, a currier, 3 cutlers, a farmer, a fuller, a gardener, 2 glaziers, a grocer, a hatter, 2 hedgers, 4 innkeepers, a joiner, 18 labourers, 4 maltsters, 3 masons, a pattern maker, a plumber, 2 postboys, a rat catcher, 3 sawyers, a shopkeeper, 2 sievers, 2 tailors, a thatcher, a thresher and a wheelwright.[3]

The cloth industry was Wessex's largest user of labour until the early 19th century. Mention has been made of the passage through Hindon of waggons carrying serges to London. Hindon was not a centre of production, but seems to have had some people involved in processing for enterprises elsewhere. There were probably a few, who would have been young females, involved in silk throwing (spinning) for the Jupe family in Mere. This had faded out by the end of the century, but some involvement in the linen dowlas and bed-tick industry in Mere and elsewhere survived longer.[4]

Glove making was also a west country industry and glovers and curriers are listed above. A tannery in Hindon provided for them, as for boot and shoe makers in the 19th century.[5]

There were at least six clockmakers in Hindon in the century. Why Hindon should have become such a centre is not clear, but it may be that craftsmen migrated from Salisbury, where clockmaker/ gunsmiths worked in numbers. Two or three Brachers worked here. A John Bracher made the long case cottage clock shown in Pl. 16. George Steevens (1716-1806) is recorded with Sun Insurance Co. as 'gunsmith, clockmaker and victualler' in 1759. His will is preserved.[6] He made the 'lantern' clock illustrated (Pl. 17), with a 30-hour 'birdcage' movement and an endless chain or rope pendulum arrangement that allows one weight to power both time and strike. The unanswered question is how did it emigrate to Australia?

Plate 16 (left). Long case cottage clock by
John Bracher, made 1765-1780 [courtesy of
Mrs. S. Whatley]
Plate 17 (above). Lantern clock by George
Steevens, 1716-1806 [courtesy of Melbourne
Clock Museum]

Most jobs in this period, however, must have derived from the
coach, chaise, carriage and cart business and the horses that drew it.
The number of inns and alehouses that supported the trade has
always fascinated local residents and the glossy magazines – 14, says
the newspaper account of the Fire. Hudson (see below) says 13, and
Sheard seems to do the same. This writer has read or heard of 16

alleged names of pubs, of which he has found documentary reference to 14, two of which may be a duplication (Appdx. D). They certainly did not all exist at the same time. Pubs then as now failed, and were revived; many were burnt or damaged, and restored. Part of the problem is the old official distinction, often blurred, between inns and alehouses. Both go back a long way. Some inns were founded in the 12th and 13th centuries, although the earliest surviving structural remains belong to the 16th. An inn became defined as a substantial hostelry on a major route, required to provide accommodation for travellers relative to traffic demands, and offering food, wine, beer and spirits. By the stage coach period they often became smartish social gathering places, and venues for local business such as market trading, auctions, banking and sessions of magistrates' courts. In Hindon's case winter church vestry meetings tended to migrate to the warmth of the better establishments. Big innkeepers were expert in business, formed an economic elite, and often belonged to family dynasties.

Alehouses were the distant ancestors of the most basic English pub today or in the recent past, offering ale and beer (later spirits) and basic food. They often operated in private houses and cottages with just a tap room or cellar, and not necessarily all year round. Market and fair days would be their mainstay, and a good deal of their business would be of the 'jug and bottle' variety – taking daily refreshment to the many workshops in the town. Both inns and alehouses were required by statute to be licensed, and magistrates were supposed to enforce this. Naturally, this was seized upon with gusto by puritan justices in Wiltshire in the 1640s as an excuse to order the suppression of all illicit houses. However in the more relaxed 18th century licenses were granted more freely.[7] In Hindon's case it is not easy to follow the licensed history of every establishment; indeed not always clear as to what is an inn and what an alehouse. This chapter will briefly feature the more significant inns the sites of which can still be identified today. Appendix D will list the remaining pub names which are recorded, and on which detailed study might follow.

The Lamb Inn, as we saw in the previous chapter, was a main host to the stage coach trade in the 18th and 19th centuries. As such, with the night-time stops it had to be a 24-hour operation; with relays of chamberlains, grooms, ostlers, stable boys, tapsters, cooks – chambermaids! A major employer in the town. In the 18th and 19th centuries it was the venue for JPs Petty and almost certainly Quarter Sessions.[8] It advertised in the *Salisbury & Winchester Journal* in 1785 for the hire of, 'neat post-chaises with able horses and careful drivers at shortest notice' – this a year before Pitt's discomfiture, maybe at this inn! The present L-shaped, mid-18th century building is mainly of limestone ashlar with tiled roof. Its pretensions to gentility can be seen in the main hotel entrance, a fine pedimented door case with anthemion frieze and half-glazed double doors. An elegant bow window lies to its left. There is a stable yard to the east, and extensive cellars, in three separate units, underneath. These were surveyed by Ron Wilson and others in 2002-3, and revealed a labyrinthine arrangement totalling an area of 1327 square feet in all. This may not all have been in use in every period, but it gives some idea of the amount of stock that needed to be stored by such enterprises.

Opposite the Lamb across the north end of the lower High Street lay the Swan Inn, the only other house known to have serviced the stage coach trade, as we have seen. A 3-storey building with massive internal timbers, a cellar and a yard behind, but no architectural sophistication, it traded as an inn until about the 1860s. It had been put up for sale on a change of ownership in 1787, when the following household goods were advertised:

> ten feather beds, with bedsteads and hangings, quilts and blankets, four
> deal dining tables, with other tables, pewter, pots and bowles, compass
> settle, eight day clock, kitchen grate and kitchen furniture.[9]

Clearly a comfortable berth. It later became Rawlings' store, and is currently divided into three private houses.

Further down the lower High Street are several archways leading to lanes giving access to the fields to the west. The present Queen's Head Cottage, Apple Tree Cottage and Queen's Head Mews front a cobbled courtyard that leads to the fields. This was the site of the Queen's Head Inn where carriers called en-route to Warminster in the 1850s. There is a cellar of 350 square feet below Apple Tree Cottage.

To the north across the present B3089 lies the Angel Inn previously mentioned, first recorded thus in 1711 but renamed the Grosvenor Arms between the mid 1830s and 2001. A fine 18th century building of rendered brick with chamfered rusticated quoins and hipped tile roof, it has a well preserved sequence of contemporary storerooms and stable buildings on the north side of its partly walled courtyard. No record has been seen to suggest that it handled the stage coaching trade. We have noted that north-south carriage trade called here in 1875, and there is a photo, currently missing, showing what seem to be farmers in its courtyard on market day. Cellar area is today about 165 square feet, consistent with the needs of a smaller inn.

Facing the Angel across the upper High Street is the Post Office stores, which was Standford White's bakery in the early 20th century, and before that the Crown Inn. Built about 1700 it is of dressed limestone in two storeys with a half-hipped roof.[10] The cellar covers about 475 square feet. In 1848 various carriers operating between Salisbury, Shaftesbury, Wincanton, Sherborne, Yeovil, Exeter, Bristol, Mere and Bath called here weekly.[11] The Crown ceased operating in the 1850s.

An example of an inn-keeping dynasty was the Beckett family. In the 1780s John Beckett held the Swan, his son John the Queen's Head, and William Beckett the Red Lyon Inn. Another William held the Red Lion in 1830.[12] Archibald Beckett of the same family developed many commercial properties in Tisbury later in that century. He built the Benett Arms and the former brewery in Church Street, which delivered its product in the village by horse-drawn dray.

The names of most of these pubs are conventional, but that of the Lamb deserves some mention. We saw above that the name of the Angel might have had origin in the dedication of the first chapel. 'The Lamb' may of course, be a reference merely to the droving trade, but we shall see in the next chapter that the later dedication of the old chapel and that of the present church has been to St. John the Baptist. A very worn panel over the west door shows the Agnus Dei, medieval emblem of Christ the Lamb of God, which has been echoed in recent paintings of the inn's hanging sign. The medieval mind, lacking scientific methods of observation and analysis represented everything religious in terms of symbols. Thus the Baptist was usually shown in desert garb pointing to the Lamb, or carrying a book showing the Agnus Dei. In time he came to be regarded as the protector of all those involved in the wool trade. Might this be the origin of the pub's name?[13]

19th Century : Land, Landlords, Buildings

The century opened with Calthorpe still the major landowner in Hindon, but with Beckford, whose estate in Fonthill Gifford parish then ran down to the Dene at the southern end of the town, buying property. He had started this in 1789. LTAs show him to have owned 32 properties by 1796, 36 by 1808, some bought from Calthorpe. In 1783 he was endowing a school in Hindon.[1] There is no doubt that his building ambitions provided much work for labourers and skilled craftsmen in the area. He began work on the fantastical Fonthill Abbey on Hinckley Hill about 1790. The cyclopean task of building the seven-mile wall around the estate (Beckford, a modern man in some respects, wanted to keep out the local hunt) is said to have pressed into service every cart in the neighbourhood. Apart from providing work, Beckford became 'a caring and responsible landlord at Fonthill whose departure in 1822 was still regretted 20 years later . . . by the cottagers.' He 'staged hugely popular football matches at Fonthill and encouraged rural sports.'[2]

His entertainment of Vice-Admiral Lord Nelson, victor of the Nile and another social misfit, with Emma and William Hamilton in the sepulchral gloom of the unfinished Abbey at Christmas 1800 is well known. Less so is his more democratic Twelfth Night party of 1797, held in front of Fonthill Splendens, the Alderman's Palladian palace down by the lake, that was later quarried for the Abbey.[3] This was to celebrate and encourage progress in the building of the Abbey, and generally to show off. Two huge bonfires were lit before Splendens that burned into the small hours. Between them a Turkish tent for Beckford and gentry, including Salisbury's Mayor and corporation members. Half moons of tables for the children's lunch. A large marquee with seven tables, each sitting 100 local tenants and villagers who came by ticketed invitation, for whom an ox and ten sheep were roasted on eleven barbecues. Outside, bread and strong beer for 10,000 of 'the multitude of strangers who were admitted to the park.' After lunch wrestling, races, single-stick contests and a football match watched by them, and after dark, roast beef for the gentry in the house washed down by 30 gallons of punch and fine wines.[4]

Nothing like it has been seen here since, but such goings-on, and the expense of building the Abbey could not last forever. Beckford, eventually broke, sold up to John Farquar in 1822 to go and build another tower on Lansdown Hill in Bath. Farquar, of humble origins, had made a fortune manufacturing gunpowder for the government of India under Warren Hastings. He was not quite as eccentric as Beckford, but he was very deaf. He failed to hear the collapse of the Abbey tower about his ears in 1825. He left, and his holdings in Hindon seem to have been bought by Richard Grosvenor, then Lord Belgrave and to succeed his father as 2nd Marquess of Westminster in 1845.[5] He held 33 properties in the borough in 1826, and 35, to Calthorpe's 92, in 1832.[6] One of these was the Angel Inn, which was re-named the Grosvenor Arms by 1838, when it was sold to James Morrison (q.v.). Grosvenor, after prolonged legal tangles, sold the Fonthill Estate, including Hindon properties to Morrison in 1838. But records are either confusing or missing and appear to show Westminster, as he now was, buying property again in Hindon which he gave to his daughter Lady Octavia Grosvenor when she married Sir Michael Shaw-Stewart, Bt. in 1852.[7]

We have seen that the old Anglican free chapel of Hindon received a charter from Mary Tudor in 1558. That operated for a couple of centuries, but then fell into disuse through death and failure to appoint new governors. The citizens petitioned George III, who in 1779 appointed fresh governors and renewed the grant under similar conditions.[8] The relevant document is the first so far seen that refers to the chapel's dedication to St. John, Baptist, but it is likely that this goes back earlier, possibly to the Restoration of 1660.[9] The building, which had been developed in stone in the usual pragmatic medieval way, survived to be painted by John Buckler (1770-1851) in 1804. A copy of this watercolour hangs in the present church. The Calthorpe map of 1748 and the Tithe Apportionment map of 1844 show the land that was held by the chapel at those times. The building was, however, dilapidated and various repairs in the 1830s and 1840s seem to have been fairly flimsy. Nor was the building ordered according to mid-Victorian High Church concepts.[9] In 1869 the long dependence of the chapelry on East Knoyle was severed. Hindon became a separate ecclesiastical parish, and the living a vicarage. The old chapel (Pl. 18) was demolished and the present church, designed by T. H. Wyatt (1807-1880), built 1870-1. The estimated cost of £3,100 was guaranteed by Westminster, who did not live to see its completion.

The question of glebe is considered in Appdx. E.

James Morrison (1789-1857) is one of the more interesting of landlords in the area. He was grandson to George, reputedly by origin a Scottish drover, who kept, appropriately, the George Inn at Middle Wallop, Hampshire, on a droving route and at the first horse-change on the Salisbury to Andover coaching route. James' origins were therefore in a place of similar character to Hindon's.

Aged 18, he hitched a lift on a coach to London and got a job as shopman for a haberdasher in the City. By 25 he was a partner and had married the boss's daughter. He was an early exponent of the principle of 'small profits and quick returns', and of targeting sellers

Plate 18. Hindon old chapel, about 1850-60. The present Post Office is on the right. The intervening buildings have gone. [Photo: HVA]

rather than buyers. Business soared. Highly intelligent, an avid reader, he fell in with some of the leading Radicals of the day, Jeremy Bentham, Francis Place, the poet Southey and Robert Owen, in this way also fitting in with Hindon's Whig tradition. He was elected MP for St. Ives in 1830, but after the Reform Act of 1832 transferred to Ipswich. He may have visited Fonthill with his parents in December 1800 to see the building works and gape at the Nelson visit. He may also have known Burton Pynsent. In 1829 he stayed at the Pavilion at Fonthill, the only surviving wing of Splendens. In 1830 he agreed to buy it and the surrounding park, although legal complications delayed completion for some time. Thereafter he was a good landlord, visited every spring and autumn with his own family, and made many ornamental alterations to the Pavilion grounds and lake. He held a 'Reform Festival' on the 'Terraces' in 1832, and when in residence sat on Hindon's quarter session bench.[10]

James Morrison left the estate to his second son Alfred (1821-1897), a very different man, many-sided, connoisseur, collector, patron of craftsmen, agriculturalist and sponsor of field sports. The terrier for the Fonthill Estate in 1892 lists 42 properties in Hindon, including the Grosvenor Arms Hotel and Queen's Head Yard (the inn itself having closed by 1891). After Alfred's death most of these including the Grosvenor and Queen's Head Yard were sold.

19th Century: Conflict and Decline

The comparative prosperity of towns on coaching routes could not disguise the generally depressed condition of agricultural labourers after the long years of the Napoleonic wars (1803-1815). Although not worse off in nominal monetary terms than their pre-war predecessors, they were in poor shape, and many were only kept from starvation by the poor rate. Hindon became entangled in an explosion of anger in 1830 that involved it in its most violent recorded incident.

We saw in 'Parliament 1700-1832' that the complacent belief that the parliamentary borough system fairly represented local interests began to be eroded, particularly among the Whigs, who had lacked a majority between 1815 and 1830. Bad harvests in 1828-31 exacerbated long festering discontent. The French staged a peaceful revolution in July 1830 that ousted the Bourbons. In that year there was widespread disturbance in a total of 16 counties of England, mainly in the south, protesting at the poverty of agricultural labourers, whose weekly wage could be as little as five to nine shillings. It took the form of smashing the new threshing machines, seen as depriving the poor of the winter work of threshing with the flail, all that was left after farmers paid off labourers at the end of harvest.

Market day in Hindon on 2 December 1830 was, as always, on Thursday. By this time the traditional wares on sale had been augmented by agricultural machinery, particularly threshers. William Henry Hudson, naturalist and writer, brought up on the South American pampas, became a struggling journalist and author in London. Near the end of his life he stayed at the Lamb Inn for part of 1909 while writing his classic 'A Shepherd's Life'. He was just in time to record the memory of an old man of 89 who had witnessed the event:

> He was but a small boy, attending the Hindon school, when the rioters appeared on the scene, and he watched their entry from the schoolhouse window. . . the market was stopped by the invaders, and the agricultural machines brought for sale and exhibition were broken up. The picture that remains in his mind is of a great excited crowd in which men and cattle and sheep were mixed together in the wide street.... and, of shouting and noise of smashing machinery, and finally the mob pouring forth over the down on its way to the next village, he and other little boys following their march.

The next village was Tisbury, and thence to Pyt House, 4½ miles south of Hindon, owned by John Benett, a progressive farmer who had installed threshing machines and was much hated in the neighbourhood as a result. After an initially conciliatory confrontation, Benett was felled by a thrown stone, the rioters proceeding to smash machines at two of his farms.

Returning to Tisbury, the rioters were intercepted by the Hindon Troop of the Yeoman Cavalry of Wiltshire, a unit resulting from Pitt's creation of a home defence and anti-riot force at the start of the French revolutionary wars. They were an establishment bunch recruited from local worthies, squires and farmers; obliged to 'find their own horses, saddles and leather breaches (each Horse to be fourteen Hands and a half high, or upwards).'[1] Another example of the centrality of inns in local business is that the troop had been ordered to meet at the Lamb in September, in field-day order. It was commanded by Capt. William Wyndham, a local gent.[2]

On meeting the troop in a narrow place the rioters, about 500 in number, attacked it with stones, pickaxes, sledgehammers and broken bits of threshers, eventually provoking it to charge and lay about it.

Accounts of this dismal event come from different directions and vary in numbers quoted. About 25 rioters are said to have been arrested, and one labourer, Harding of Hindon, shot dead. Hudson reckoned he was killed by an excited farmer before the cavalry arrived, but at the time several locals were found to swear that the Yeomanry done it. Perhaps eight Hindonians were involved in the affray, but it is not clear whether any were charged. At trial at Salisbury Assizes, 13 rioters were sentenced to transportation for 7 years, and one for 14. In Wiltshire as a whole 154 were transported. Across southern England the totals were much higher.[3]

One lucky man was John Beckett of Hindon, clearly a stroppy fellow who might have got into trouble had not his wife locked him in the chapel tower until the commotion was over. Profiting from this unlawful arrest, he survived to be parish clerk for 60 years.[4]

These events became known as the Captain Swing riots, apparently an onomatopoeic reference to the noise made by threshing machines. There was no organised conspiracy, no linkage between regions, and very few personal attacks on farmers or landowners. The legal establishment, which in this period saw its chief function as the defence of property, took savage revenge on the poor workless. However, even at the time voices were raised to the effect that the Yeomanry had been too violent. There is no doubt that the disturbances were a significant factor in a loss of nerve by parliament that led directly to the Reform Act of 1832. The Whigs replaced the Tories. Paradoxically one of the most lordly of administrations, it viewed a concession to popular demand as the duty of a governing aristocracy. It pushed through the Bill to eventual popular approval, but never really grasped the social implications.[5] More paradoxes. John Benett, reviled landlord, believed that the agricultural crisis should be solved by representational reform carried by constitutional methods. As an MP for Wiltshire county he had presented a petition to the Commons, signed by 14,000 Wiltshire people. In March 1830 he submitted another from the corporation and burgesses of Calne, and was joined in his protest by William Cobbett, champion of the rural poor, who was arrested for sedition after the riots, but later acquitted.

The economic effects of disfranchisement on Hindon were probably not as great as has sometimes been suggested. They mainly affected the inns which had held tabs from prospective parliamentary candidates. Census returns for this period, however (Appdx. B), show a marked drop in population between an all-time high in 1831 and the next enumeration. The 1841 decrease was attributed at the time to 'emigration and the demolition of several houses', that by 1851 to 'emigration', and that by 1861 to 'migration to other parishes caused by unemployment.'[6]

The Poor Law Amendment Act of 1834 had replaced the old poor law that dated back to Elizabethan times and had ceased to work properly, with a centrally controlled system. It aimed to amalgamate parishes into poor law unions which would build workhouses regulated according to a national pattern. Hindon's inhabitants had agreed to build a new workhouse in 1812 and by the 1820s had converted a house and malthouse in the street for the purpose. In 1835 however, Hindon joined the Tisbury Poor-law Union.[7] It was later to incur severe criticism from inspectors.

These measures were claimed at the time virtually to have solved the unemployment problem in Wiltshire, but the emigration figures would seem to belie this. Certainly emigration was encouraged by local authorities; by 1836 200 people from Downton had been assisted to move to Canada, and by 1842 over 500 had emigrated from 18 villages.[8] There are other references to moves to USA, Australia and South Africa.

Internet inquiries have so far revealed two Hindon place names abroad that suggest immigration from England. In Ontario province in Canada there is a Hindon Township (an area not a town) in Haliburton County, 200 km west of Ottawa , a vast region of lakes, swamps and small townships today frequented by walkers, anglers and canoeists. In New Zealand's South Island there is an old township and station called Hindon on the Taieri Gorge Railway, 45 km north of Dunedin, Otago, now offering tourist facilities. The line had reached this point in 1889. In neither case has an individual link with our Hindon been found.

Recent personal inquiries from British Columbia have concerned Crickmays who emigrated to Canada and Australia about 1914. Numerous Crickmays appear in Hindon parish registers and census returns in the 19th century, and there are two relevant memorial headstones in the churchyard. So far the identity of the actual emigrants has not been established. In the late 1880s and 1890s some Howells belonging to a family of stonemasons went to Denver, Colorado and worked there. These contacts have been a welcome development and continue. Any readers who can contribute to this fascinating story are invited to contact the author.

Unemployment and emigration were symptoms of a general economic decline in the south-west in the 1840s and subsequently. There was a steady decline in the coach and carriage trade through Hindon, partly due to over-supply of services, which meant that many carriers went to the wall. The Fisherton Turnpike Trust's income from tolls dropped from £3,215 in 1838 to £757 in the 1860s, and it was wound up in 1870.[9] By mid-century only five or six inns or alehouses remained. The effect of railway development has already been noted. Hindon's weekly market had closed by 1889.[10]

Hudson, writing in 1909, notes how quiet Hindon had become since the busy and rumbustious days of the 18th century:

> so rustic and pretty amidst its green, swelling downs, with great woods crowning the heights beyond, that one can hardly credit . . . that it was

> formerly an important market and session town . . . that it boasted . . .
> thirteen public houses. Now it has two [Lamb and Grosvenor Arms] and
> not flourishing in these tea-and mineral-water drinking days.

The revised drinking habits must have owed much to the Temperance movement. A Primitive Band of Hope and Temperance Club was founded in Hindon about 1891. The growth of nonconformism in the 19th century may also have contributed. The Church of England chapel near the top of the High Street had reverted to Anglican liturgy at the royal Restoration of 1660, and maintained a reasonable quality of pastoral care in the not very religious 18th century. At the beginning of the 19th, protestant sects that had found fertile soil in Wiltshire from an early date and flourished during the Civil War, Commonwealth and Protectorate began to set up their own arrangements.

In Hindon this seems to have led to conflict between sections of the population. In about 1810 a philanthropic minister from Warminster, influenced by Mrs. Joanna Turner, a founder of dissenting chapels in the area, built a Congregationalist chapel in the east Dene. The construction was said to have been opposed by the mainstream Anglicans, and that men on horseback were deployed to resist obstruction of the work by them. In 1840 the Primitive Methodists, a breakaway from the mainstream Wesleyan Methodists, and deriving much support from the rural poor, bought a plot in a field to the west of the upper High Street, and were, again, it is said, grievously obstructed in the building work of a new chapel. Worship continued there for many years, with at one time a congregation of 90 and a Sunday school of 70.[11]

It has to be said that the accounts of these conflicts derive mainly from nonconformist sources. Nonetheless, it is clear that there were internal conflicts within the village that lingered for some time.

Hudson, wonderful observer and recorder, also tells us what he was told about the smuggling trade in mid-century. There is no doubt that contraband wine, spirits and cosmetics smuggled from France into Dorset coves, found their way up through places like Hindon, to be fenced and moved eastwards and into the midlands. Local reference libraries have no records of this specific to Hindon, but consider that Hudson is likely to be accurate in saying that Hindon was involved. He tells the engaging story of a small farmer and carrier in the village who never left his house and work but stored contraband beneath his manure heap and pigsty. Every so often his blind son would drive his old mother in his father's cart to Salisbury to deliver little parcels to recipients who had ordered contraband goods. This all went wrong when a mistaken delivery was made, and the conscientious twit of a recipient made earnest enquiries as for whom the delivery was intended, with dire consequences. Ewart White, who farmed in the area until his death in 1975, claimed that one of his ancestors was Silas White, a well known smuggler in the early 19th century. The cellars of the Lamb Inn were said to be the hiding place for his illicit goods, which he took in his carrier's cart to Bath.[12]

Such, no doubt basically reliable tales, have led to occasional legends in Hindon that tunnels beneath and across the High Street exist, or existed to shuffle the little brandy barrels from one side to the other to avoid the excise men when they came to inspect. These are much loved and repeated by the glossies. Some trouble has been taken in compiling this account to examine the likelihood that they are true. A working party of ten surveyed 27 of the perhaps 35 cellars below houses in the High Street for two purposes: to attempt to locate, by the size of cellars, the lost inns and alehouses, and to find any evidence of old tunnels. The first was inconclusive. The second established without doubt that there is no such evidence and the results are summarized in Appendix F.

The W.I. scrapbook of 1956 preserves two stories redolent of the atmosphere of the mid 19th century. A lad who was employed to clean out the many wells down the village street was betrayed by a

faulty rope, and fell. It took some time to haul him back up, and
when his head eventually emerged above ground he inquired 'Be oi
'urt?'. The second concerns two Italians who brought a dancing bear
into the village, announcing their arrival by blowing a tinny trumpet
and beating a drum. This noise so enraged a local dog that it ran out
and bit the animal in the foot. Poor bear treed herself, and could only
be persuaded to come down when offered a dish of beer. The past is
a foreign country.

By the time that Hudson, 68, stayed, the place had changed. In
1907 the Lamb advertised itself as offering 'good accommodation for
motorists and cyclists'. Hudson would have come by train to
Tisbury, and pedalled his bike the three miles to Hindon. Indeed, he
is so imagined by an anonymous *Times* feature writes in the 1960s
(easier to imagine then than now):

> On any quiet afternoon in Hindon it is not difficult to imagine that it is
> still 1909, that the steps you hear on the stairs at the Lamb are those of
> an elderly visitor from Westbourne Park who is being shown up to his
> room and that in the conversation which sounds but faintly from .... the
> long landing he is asking the innkeeper to watch for the cart of the
> Tisbury carrier, who will be bringing his trunk from the station.[13]

So the century draws calmly to a close, with Hudson, just five
years before Armageddon, describing his beloved birds from an
open window in the Lamb:

> . . . we had three pairs of birds, throstle, pied wagtail and flycatcher –
> breeding in the ivy covering the wall facing the village street, just over
> my window. I watched them when building, incubating, feeding their
> young, and bringing their young off. . . The last to come off were the
> flycatchers, on 18 June. It was the morning of the day I left, and one of
> the little things flitted into the room where I was having my breakfast. I
> succeeded in capturing it before the cats found out, and put it back on
> the ivy. There were three young birds; I had watched them from the time
> they hatched, and when I returned a fortnight later, there were the

Plate 19. The Lamb Inn, from a postcard [enhanced by R. McColl]

three, still being fed by their parents in the trees and on the roof, their favourite perching-place being on the swinging sign of the 'Lamb'.' (Plate 19).

War

In Hindon's church porch are inscribed the names of 118 men who went to the Great War, of whom 18 did not return: names of the latter are also on the war memorial. This out of a total population of 405 at the 1911 census enumeration. It gives some idea of the evisceration of the old English countryside in that conflict. What is striking about these lists is the number of surnames that go back in Hindon records for centuries. Of merely those there listed, this writer has seen references to Bevis, Burt, Bye, Doughty, Dukes and Ingram going back to the 18th century; Baker, Becket, Phillips, Pitman, Ranger, Snook, Stevens and White to the 17th, and Hacker (the name probably means woodcutter) to the early 14th.

At the outbreak of war in 1914 there was a great increase of traffic on the railway system in Wiltshire, mainly to get troops from the newly built training camps on the Plain to the embarkation port of Southampton. Special military lines were built, including one from the Codford area up to the downs.[1] However there does not seem to be any information specific to Hindon in the published material.[2]

The Second World War (WWII) was another matter. Only three Hindonians fell, but the village was in the middle of what became a vast armed camp in the gradual build-up of British and allied forces prior to D-Day. Before that, the area had seen the re-grouping of troops rescued from Dunkirk. The railway station at Semley was very busy at this time. E. T. G. Mortland of Selsey, E.

Sussex, then in the 2nd Bn., Grenadier Guards recalls a visit to the unit by Montgomery, then commander of V Corps in defence of Hampshire and Dorset against the expected imminent invasion. He was asked if two junior officers whose wives had just given birth could be granted leave to visit them. 'I have no room for any sentimentality in my army!', he cried. Leave refused, and in that desperate period, quite rightly.

In October 1940 the *Western Gazette* reported that four crew members of a Dornier 17 that had been on a bombing mission 'got into difficulties' over Hindon and baled out, landing safely over a spread of 12 miles. One presented himself to Chicklade Bottom Farm; the local policeman was called and took charge of him. Another knocked on the door of a bungalow occupied by Mrs. Furnell (now replaced by 'Upwey' or 'Crow's Top' just outside Hindon to the west). Uncertain of the procedure to be adopted in such situations, she directed him to the village but, confused in the blackout, he walked in the wrong direction, and after snatching a few hours' sleep under a hayrick, was picked up by some county council roadmen. The other two surrendered at a farmhouse. The plane, meanwhile, flew doggedly on in a straight line for 160 miles until it ran out of fuel and subsided gently into the Stour mud flats near Ipswich. The pilot, Leutnant Werdemann, when questioned, said that he could not understand why his craft had flown on so far. He was concerned about the fate of his suitcase, which was plucked out of the marshes by a naval rating. One suspects that the crew had already grown tired of the war.

On 20 December 1940 a stick of three bombs fell in late afternoon in fields across the road to the north east past the present Glebe Farm to the A303, then known as the Wylye Road. One left a crater as big as a house, and the concussion from another blew two soldiers off their bicycles. It was thought that the target had been a searchlight near Chicklade. Allen Bunch, now of Andover but a boy of ten at the time, recalls that he had to walk to school in Hindon from Chicklade and that there was a searchlight unit billeted in tents on the hill towards Hindon. There were also soldiers with horses in tents in a field belonging to the school. Readers may care to note two strange concrete cylinders now built into the Angel Inn's courtyard stonework. These are said to have been part of a primitive anti-tank defence in the early days of the war to prevent an incursion of panzers from the Mere road.

It is impossible now to reconstruct completely what units and divisions of units were stationed here at any particular time. Nissen huts and other structures sprouted in the village and the surrounding fields and woods. Troops were billeted, came and went. In early 1941 Churchill decreed that a Guards Armoured Division should be formed. Units of it trained in this area: battalions of the Welsh, Grenadier and Scots Guards at Codford, the Coldstream towards Heytesbury[3], and the 2nd (Armoured) Battalion, Irish Guards in Fonthill Park, the men in nissen huts at the top end and the tanks in what became known as the Irish sheds at the bottom. They were there from September 1941 to the autumn of 1942, when they moved to Warminster. They recall:

> We were very happy at Fonthill Gifford . . . The camp . . . had been built by refugees from Germany. They gave concerts, and among them we discovered an Austrian tailor who had represented Meyer and Mortimer in Vienna. He did a roaring trade in service dress jackets and trousers. From these people we first heard of the horrors of concentration camps – which we were to witness later at Sandbostel.[4]

During this time Hindon's war memorial, which then stood just south of the road crossing at The Square (Pl. 20), was demolished by a runaway tank. Some say fully crewed, it went out of control at the top of the High Street, careered across the road junction, knocked down the memorial, maybe four trees and a water standpipe, finally coming to rest against another tree. Fortunately, there were no casualties. There has been a recent local tendency to

Plate 20. The War Memorial and Rawlings shop in the late 1930s. The right hand side of the building enclosing seven windows has since been demolished to give better vehicular access to Angel Lane, now arbitrarily renamed 'Mere Road' [photo: Rawlings & Sons]

blame this on the Americans, which seems fair enough, except that the evidence is against it. The aftermath of the accident was witnessed by John Snook, then a boy of 10, and confirmed by Jim Farnell and Stan Withey, who later served with the light infantry in north-west Europe. They confirm that the Irish were responsible. Or rather, that the tank, a Mark V Cruiser or Covenanter, was. Designed and built, for some reason, by the LMS Railway Company from 1937, under-armed, under-armoured and mechanically unreliable, it has been described by the archivist of the Bovington Tank Museum as 'arguably the worst tank ever issued to the British Army', which, considering the quality of vehicles in which our people were expected to fight for most of WW II, is saying quite a lot. It had a highly complicated, hydraulically-operated steering system that, particularly with trainee drivers, could produce the disconcerting effect at certain speeds, and particularly in reverse, that a pull on a steering lever had the vehicle going in the opposite direction to that intended. This may have been the cause of the accident here, or maybe the clutch failed, or anything. The Guards in Codford and Wylye caused similar damage to buildings, particularly on corners, and we have to absolve 'The Micks' of any blame. They went on to noble deeds in Normandy, Belgium and north-west Germany with considerable casualties and we owe them our affection and respect.

The build-up of American forces in Bristol and the west country, codenamed Op. BOLERO, began during 1943. British units like the Irish Guards had been moved east and north so as to avoid the crossing of communication lines. From Cheltenham to Bournemouth and from Exeter to Swindon, countless small packets of units of the eventual US 1st Army were posted in bewildering fragmentation. In September 1943 arrived the US 3rd Armored (Spearhead) Division, initially an independent formation that came under 1st Army command after the Normandy landings. Commemorative plaques in Mere and East Knoyle record elements that were billeted there, but the Irish Guards were the only unit training round Hindon that had actual tanks. Lists show that the 23rd Armored Engineer Battalion of 3rd Armored was billeted at 'Fonthill Bishop', presumably in Fonthill Park, which may explain why local recollection is confused as to whether there were tanks or not. There were also five Ordnance units, from battalion to company strength on Great Ridge. John Snook also recalls Americans camped in the thorn scrub to the west of the village, at the time much more extensive than now, that may have been 215th Signals Depot Company and 295th Engineer Battalion 'C' of XIX Corps, that are mentioned in the lists as camped in 'Hindon'.[5]

Also on the Ridge there were some Italian and German prisoners of war. The Italians, about 20 in number, came from the Western Desert, and worked in the old sawmills there (Pl. 21). Later they were allowed to drive tractors. Jim Farnell recalls that on their arrival in the area they were dropped off on the present A303, and drifted up in the hill in twos and threes, with the rifle of the British pioneer corporal in charge of them being carried by one of them. In contrast, the 20 or so Germans, who arrived later, formed themselves up under own command, and marched up as a squad. They, however, were also glad to get out of the war.

Plate 21. Italian prisoners of war at the old sawmills on Great Ridge. At the back on the left is Stan Farnell, with Hugh Ponton beside him. The three in front are all Italians, with Alessandro Gabriani on left.

Off duty Americans often congregated in Hindon, and would sit on the remains of the war memorial and whistle the girls. A canteen was opened at the rear of the Methodist chapel in the High Street (until recently a craft shop), run by Ivy Fry, which is remembered as a home from home for American servicemen. Serving tea, biscuits and cake, there were also cards, darts, draughts, chess and a billiard table borrowed from the reading room (now the village hall). Dances were held on base or in the British Legion or W.I. huts in Hindon.

There was at least one serious and lasting romance. Norman Anderson, a sergeant in the US medical corps, met Edward Jerrim's daughter Grace, a nurse from Oxford, at a canteen in Fonthill. They married in 1945 and lived happily in Potsdam, New York for many years.

The Americans, as we all know, came laden with supplies, especially of food, that had been denied to the locals for years. The rationing laws were so strictly enforced that, when US units moved on, they were usually compelled to burn or bury surplus stock. Enterprising small boys could sometimes liberate small amounts of this; no names, no pack-drill. The big exception was immediately before D-Day. Secrecy had been so tight that no locals knew of the date. An American, Corporal Stark, who used to attend chapel services on Sunday nights, one night asked if he could sing a solo, and rendered 'Rock of Ages' in a fine voice. Later he went up to the Old Bakery and asked Albert Hayter to cook him bacon and eggs. He was never seen again, and next morning Fonthill Park was deserted of troops and equipment, but by no means of food. The locals descended with bicycle, horse and cart, the odd car, and made free.

Much of the research for this section was done by Jenny Hedin, who mounted an exhibit of the Americans in Hindon at the celebration in July 1995 of the 50th anniversary of the end of the war. Astonishingly, tree surgeon Philip Farnell was felling beeches in Dark Walk, Fonthill Stud Paddocks only a day or two before, and removed several pieces of bark carrying carvings done by troops in that period. These formed part of the exhibition (Plate 22).

Plate 22. Bark carvings by allied servicemen, WWII [Photo: K. Gigiel]

It remains to recount the exploits of Hindon people in the campaigns of the Royal Wiltshire Yeomanry (RWY) during the war. This was a direct successor to Pitt's Yeomanry Cavalry, of which its Hindon Troop had dispersed the Swing rioters in 1830. Since 1921 it had been part of the new Territorial Army; it saw 4½ years' active service abroad, but had rather a bitty war. In January 1940, as a trained cavalry unit, it took its 700 horses to Palestine as part of 1st Cavalry Division, but never rode them into action. With them went Captain John Morrison, grandson of Alfred. In early 1941 it was re-equipped with 15 cwt trucks as an anti-aircraft searchlight unit, and one squadron served as such in North Africa, including at Tobruk. Later, the regiment served as motorized infantry in Iraq, Syria and Persia (now Iran) in actions to deny the Germans and Vichy French forces. Morrison had at least two interesting experiences: frying an egg on the mudguard of his truck in the savage heat of Iraq, and meeting Soviet officers in Teheran, a liaison that eventually enabled huge supplies to be sent north into Russia. (Curiously, he was soon recalled by Churchill to stand as Conservative MP for Salisbury, a seat he held until 1964, when he was created Lord Margadale of Islay).

In May 1942 RWY at last got its tanks, but a motley collection of Grants, Crusaders, Shermans and trucks, fuelled variously by diesel, high and low octane petrol, and armed by weapons of nine different calibres, a quartermaster's nightmare. It joined 8th Army as part of 9th Armoured Brigade in 2nd NZ Infantry Division commanded by General Bernard Freyburg, VC.

It saw heavy action in the slogging match of the El Alamein battle in late 1942, particularly on Miteiriya Ridge and Tel Aqqaqir. This was not classic tank warfare (for which RWY were at best only half trained), but a slow business of pushing forward through minefields against superior German armour and the fearsome 88mm anti-tank guns. The regiment took heavy tank losses and over 100 casualties in all. Amid this maelstrom was Trooper Reg

Doggrell, tank driver in A Squadron, who says that his tank was the only Sherman in this action that was still mobile at its end. Armoured troops like to paint the tank's name on its side, based on battle honours or their home towns; 'Hindon' was said to be emblazoned on Doggrell's. Arthur Williams was prevented by sickness from joining the regiment for this battle but served in the subsequent advance north through Italy.

One can only admire the way these ill-equipped volunteer soldiers performed at Alamein and elsewhere. In one instance they reverted instinctively to cavalry type. At first light on 2 November 1942, B Squadron breasted a rise to be faced by a ring of 88s. To halt would have been fatal. The commander gave the order 'Charge!', and the tanks drove straight into the battery, smashing guns and killing many of their crews. A year later, when RWY were pushing up through Italy in terrible tanking country, Freyburg, great leader, sent it a message:

> We shall never forget your magnificent and decisive attack which broke enemy's guns and line on 2nd November.

It had been a second Balaclava.[6]

20th Century: Modernisation and Change

The property in Hindon that Westminster gave to his daughter Octavia on her marriage to Michael Shaw-Stewart (d. 1903) in 1852 descended to their son Walter Richard Shaw-Stewart, next owner of Fonthill Abbey Estate (centred not on Beckford's late lamented Abbey but a similarly named structure built about 1856 on the south side of Hinckley Hill). In 1922 Walter auctioned 97 properties in Hindon belonging to the estate. This marked the end of the age-old ownership of a majority of properties by owners of neighbouring estates who rented them to the inhabitants.

Cottages seem to have gone for between £40 and £90, shops for between £650 and £900, and 'houses' for figures between those two groups. The Lamb Inn was withdrawn from sale; the Grosvenor Arms, already sold by Alfred Morrison's executors, was not involved.

Those who bought the cottages were mostly poor. Basil Bevis (1908-1999) recalled in 1998 that his father, a master builder, bought the present Dolphin Cottage, probably for £110:

> We had to struggle through and pay that off and that's how life went on; sometimes you had work and sometimes you had plenty, other times you had none. That was part of the building trade – known as casual labour. It wasn't definite when the next job would come in, but you just carried on.

He recalled that after the Great War things in Hindon were 'very quiet':

> They were all agricultural people you see, and everybody worked for a farm or an estate like the Fonthill Estate, the Abbey Estate and Wyndham's estate as well as over at East Knoyle. . . so you had quite a mixture of trades . . . they either worked on the farms, or in the buildings, building anything that came along. Just 'well, I work for so and so, he's the farmer and I do whatever job comes up . . .' People never went very far . . . You went to work, you come back and dig your garden . . . You'd have a local shop which would give you so much credit . . . and then you would have to square up at the end of the week . . . Nobody had any money then, put it that way.

From this time began the installation of public utilities, many of which are noted in Appendix A. Electricity replaced the nine oil lamps in the street. The appearance of much of the landscape was changed by enclosure and arable farming that replaced sheep rearing and droving. Norah Sheard, writing in 1979, was better placed than this writer to talk to old Hindonians and recall

> . . . how the old customs have vanished; the local band [Pl. 23] and dancing in the Square: the excitement of the October fair and the woman selling sweets who set up her stall round the market cross near the church: and the days when Mr. White closed his shutters (now the PO) at eight o'clock. Gone are the days when the smell of freshly baked bread from the bakeries (Wilfrid Fry's, Mrs. Kemp's in Bakehouse Yard and others) pervaded the street. Gradually they closed down and were converted into garages. There are still Hindonians who can remember going down on Christmas Eve to Alban Lamb's house (now Albany House), . . . and collecting their share of cottage loaves . . . through a sash window in the alley way . . . working people had a right to a loaf or a part of a loaf according to the number in the family. A length of calico was also given to poor widows (Ames Charity).[1] There are those who can

remember taking cakes to be baked at Wilfrid Fry's for half a penny a cake, and a turkey to be cooked on Christmas Day . . . the Sunday afternoons or evenings when people gathered round the wells with their buckets of water to fill the copper for the Monday wash.'[2]

Plate 23. Hindon Town Band, 1930s. Edward Jerrim, Treasurer, 2nd from right, middle row

As everywhere, the end of WWII bought a swift acceleration of change. The return of service men and women and the institution of the welfare state brought new expectations and demands. The general urgent need for new housing was partly met in Hindon by the building of the council estates in East Street in 1953 and Whitehill in 1958. As members of the old families moved into these and other houses, the retired and weekenders gradually began to buy up the old cottages and renovate them. In some cases two or three were knocked into one, like present Swallow Cottage in the Dene, Daysmead and, much later, Moonfleet in the upper High Street. This did not greatly alter the external appearance of the place, and as planning and conservation controls were introduced, the chance of this happening was strangled. Currently 86 addresses, including the church, are Grade II listed, and the High Street is designated a Conservation Area.[3]

Modernisation of agriculture meant that far fewer people were employed on the land, but other opportunities opened up. During and after the war the RAF depot in the old quarries at Chilmark offered employment to many in the village. Modernisation of property gave employment to the craftsmen and builders who had always proliferated here, and in recent years the conservation standards demanded by English Heritage and the National Trust on listed buildings have led to the acquisition of many specialist skills.

Before the second world war Hindon had a blacksmith, watchmaker, window cleaner, chimney sweep, sawyer, butcher, basketmaker, cobbler, undertaker, market gardener, two fruiterers, Post Office, hardware shop, three builders, four grocers and a garage.[4] In 1939 the former Swan Inn site was occupied by Reg Rawlings' store (Pl. 24). Then employing 15 people, it sold general

Plate 24. Rawlings store, early 20th century

stores, drapery, coal, paraffin, milk, operated a paper round and could run up a made-to-measure suit. It ran a couple of charabancs taking parties to the seaside. Rawlings at one time had an eccentric advertising card:

> My business was established in 1898. I have been pleasing and displeasing people ever since. I have made money, and lost money; I have been cussed and discussed, knocked about and talked about, lied to, held up, and robbed . . . The only reason I am staying in business is to see what the hell will happen next.

Rawlings is said to have become even more eccentric and to have set light to the place in 1937. It was reconstructed with the frontage we see today. Reg's son Ed took the business over during WWII and ran it for some years. On its eventual closure it was taken over and run as an up-market delicatessen under the same name for 14 years until its final closure in 1988.

All that trade has now gone, and the only surviving retail outlet is the Post Office stores. There is nothing unusual in this change. The main causes have been new transport patterns, particularly the development of private cars, and the proliferation of large-scale merchandizing, such as supermarkets. Hindon, so quiet in Hudson's day, is back on the map. Since the late 1930s chaps in open top tourers on their way to the southwest have stopped off here for a spot of lunch. The 1950s designation of the A303 in place of the A30 as the main trunk route in that direction has greatly increased traffic, some of it to the benefit of the two pubs, a lot of it a dangerous nuisance. The railway three miles away at Tisbury carries weekly and even daily commuters to Waterloo in 100 minutes on a good day.

Let us now draw a few threads together by taking a walk down the village, starting at the top of the High Street. From here we can sense the shape of the fossilised original 13th century borough foundation, still largely intact. On the left is the modern NHS surgery, serving Hindon and 13 other villages.

Plate 25. Parish Church of St John the Baptist, Post Office stores on right
[Photo: author, 1995]

Next on the left is the Anglican church of St. John, Baptist, which we left at its building in 1870/1 (Pl. 25). Inside may be found a brief description, its history (on sale), an old photograph and a reproduction of a painting of its predecessor chapel. The ecclesiastical parish established in 1869 was enlarged in 1922 when All Saints, Chicklade, on the A303 to the north, and St. Peter's, Pertwood, in a neighbouring hamlet, were loosely combined. In 1972 this was tightened and the present parish became 'Hindon with Chicklade and Pertwood.' Various parochial reorganisations resulted in the establishment of a Tisbury Anglican Team Ministry in 1988, expanded in 2001 into the Nadder Valley Team Ministry, centred in Tisbury and including Hindon and nine other parishes, in the deanery of Chalke, the archdeaconry of Sarum and the diocese of Salisbury.

Proceeding at a dignified pace down to the crossroads, we come to the Post Office stores (ex Crown Inn) and Lamb Inn on the left, the Angel Inn and Swan House (ex Swan Inn and Rawlings) on the right, already featured above. Diverting a few yards to the left past the Lamb we come to Hindon Fellowship Club. Founded by Cecily Crisp in 1937, it is a recently refurbished and well appointed building with bar, lounge etc. that offers an alternative venue to younger and not so young villagers.

Some 65 yards down from Swan House we come to the arched entrance to a cobbled yard that was part of the Queen's Head Inn, with its mews on the left and a large shed on the right that housed its skittle alley. Continuing up the green lane brings one to Back Way from which the round barrow (Pl. 2) can just be seen on the skyline ahead. Further down the High Street on the right side the name Bank House recalls its use during the old market days. Further down, Merlin House and High Steps carry over their ground floor sash windows cement strips that are presumed to mark where awnings once extended over market stalls on the pavement.

On the left hand side Red Lion House occupies the site of the long vanished Red Lion Inn (Appendix D). Some 18th century brickwork can still be seen. No record of its usage or representation of its former appearance is known, but the cellar area of about 660 sq. ft. suggests a large establishment. Further down is the former Methodist chapel, already mentioned, that housed the canteen for American and other troops in the war.

We stop at the bottom of the street before the Dene, a winterbourne that once marked Hindon's civil parish boundary. Across it was part of Fonthill Gifford parish, and in Beckford's day, although he owned property in Hindon also, his own territory stopped here. We have seen that Hindon was in the *ecclesiastical* parish of East Knoyle until 1869, when it achieved independence. The emergence of separate *civil* parishes is obscure, but by late Tudor times church vestries had assumed certain duties that we would now regard as local government responsibilities, such as poor relief, highway maintenance and minor law and order matters. These duties would have usually covered the same geographical areas as the *ecclesiastical* parishes, but the Local Government Act of 1894 that created 14,000-odd *civil* parishes in England and Wales, including Hindon, often changed that. The Victorians are greatly to be blamed for using the same term, 'parish', to describe both types of council area; even fine minds, concentrating on other matters, are known to have become confused. Hindon's civil parish extended to the north as far as the Ox Drove, but did not include Chicklade and Pertwood, which the church one did. In 1934 a reorganisation of civil boundaries brought the houses south of the Dene and up to the wooded slopes beyond, together with outlying parts of Chicklade and Berwick St. Leonard, into Hindon civil parish, adding 110 more residents and thereafter comprising 1031 acres or 417 hectares.

If after all this we are still standing before the Dene, we look across to the building on the left before the road up to Tisbury, the present village hall. Between 1867 and 1889 it was called Sessions Hall, and housed the Petty and probably the Quarter Sessions. In 1889 the Sessions were moved to Tisbury.[5] In the 1922 sale the hall was bought and given to the village by Hugh Morrison, son of Alfred and father of John Morrison, becoming a reading room providing a venue for men, often unemployed, to have access to newspapers and other material. Its viability was eroded by the Fellowship Club in the late 1930s.

To the right of the village hall is an 18th century building that was used as a 'mad house' from 1790 or earlier (not Dene House as suggested by Sheard). Treatment of 'lunatics' until well into the 19th century was more concerned with confinement and restraint than care and treatment. All asylums had to be licensed, and the smaller ones visited by a physician, surgeon or apothecary twice a week. This was one of 11 in Wiltshire, and had a good record at inspections. Operating until 1844, it had a maximum number of inmates of 23 in 1828. Pl. 26, a rather crude drawing, shows that it had a walled enclosure with cottages and other buildings used as day or sleeping rooms. No divine services were held, but

Plate 26. The 'mad house', about 1832. The present village hall is to the left of the 18th-century house where the tree is shown here. The Dene in foreground. [From a drawing in W&SRO A1/562/4]

> such as require Bibles, prayer Books or other unsophisticated good works are supplied with them. [Amusements were provided by a hand organ and cards,] as well as canary and other singing birds for those who are attached to such domesticated living objects.[6]

Later the building housed the police superintendent, while two constables lived in the white-painted cottages adjoining. The cells, now gone, were to the right. The police station moved to Tisbury in 1889.

Turning left into School Lane we are now following Jackson's suggested line of the old Saxon herepath. The school building itself dates from 1854 when it was founded as a C of E school by Octavia Shaw-Stewart, but the first record of any school is of the younger Beckford endowing a free school in 1783.[7] By 1818 it was still going, together with another supported by Calthorpe, and three dames schools for small children. Various changes occurred during the 19th century. In 1921 the existing schools came under the local education authority. In 1972 Hindon's became a C of E Aided First School. With declining numbers it merged with East Knoyle's as St. Mary's and St. John's School, at Hindon. Following education authority changes in 2003 it has become a C of E voluntary aided primary school. Current number of pupils is about 30.[8]

Retrospect – a Personal View

Hindon has largely owed its survival as a viable community, so far for about 785 years, to themes that we have followed in this account: its proximity to through trunk routes; the compactness of the original town plantation (that engenders a feeling that this is a close place where people look out for each other), and the old continuity of family occupation. Perhaps less so with the last; through history people have come here to find work, but also left for the same reason. This continuity must inevitably become further diluted over time.

Survival has never occurred without change. From the feudal bishops' initial commercial venture; through long years as a fruitful market and fair site; land ownership passing to gentry whose class represented it in parliament for nearly 400 years; from prosperity in the coaching age that spawned a proliferation of trades and skills and much business activity, to comparative stagnation but still virtual self-sufficiency in the 19th century. Perhaps the future may see as the most fundamental change of all the shift since the second world war from a producing community to a largely residential one. The arrival in the last few years of a number of younger people working from home may dilute this trend, but a trend it remains. It may be exacerbated by the recent absurd rise in price of the older properties, which may be affordable only by the well-heeled retired.

About a quarter of the population live on the council estates, but a number own their properties, which consequently do not often come on the market.

This book is history, not prophecy, and we cannot predict future governments' policies towards the countryside. But Hindon does not give the feeling of a society in decline. Crafts and skills that have always existed here have been inherited and are now deployed in other areas. Post war arrivals have contributed to a significant upgrading of the older housing stock. Social amenities survive. The village seems unanimous that, despite sometimes bewildering changes in management and style it has room, with the passing trade, for two pubs. The usual clubs, associations and social groupings pursue active lives (Appendix A). WI, Royal British Legion, Fellowship Club, Horticultural Show, Whist Drive, coffee mornings, charity sales, bell-ringing, keep-fit classes, painting circles proliferate. The children's playground is maintained and a major effort is currently being made to revivify the old council allotments. Hindon is an indefatigable and virtuoso raiser of quite startling amounts of money for a variety of local and wider causes.

The most striking feature of this village to the writer, who came here 15 years ago, is that there seems to be a sense of corporate identity and of belonging. It is notable how many new arrivals say that they moved here without quite knowing why, but soon began to feel that they were intended to do so.

*Plate 27. View from the Dene up High Street, c. 1860. Note wellhead
on the right*

Plate 28. The same view, 1950s [Photo: Kirby, Tisbury]

*Plate 29. High Street, about 1905. Grosvenor Arms on right. The van
belonged to a launderers in Tisbury.*

*Plate 30. Tree pollarding in lower High Street, about 1905. Note pony and
trap and heavier horse with traditional farm cart. Trap has A. Hayter
painted on the side. [Enhancement by R McColl]*

Plate 31. Maypole on Mr. Potter's ground, c. 1920. Mary Ford, Queen.

Plate 32. Outing, 1923 [Photo: HVA]

Plate 34. James Knowles, butcher, outside his shop, now Queen's Head Cottage, with Len and Cathie, 1913. Note weighplate in foreground.

Plate 33. James Oliver, shepherd (1844-1936), on Two Mile Down in early 1920s, after retirement, in borrowed smock. The sheep may be Hampshire Downs. Described as 'a cussed old chap' by his descendants.

Plate 35. Hindon School, c. 1930, from school grounds looking north. Miss V. Andrew, teacher. Behind, at left, rear of Greystones on High Street. At right angles to it Jubilee Buildings, then ten dwellings. Long low building behind Miss Andrew demolished after WWII and replaced by bungalows. School Lane can be seen beyond fence, middle distance. [Photo: Scholastic Souvenir Co., Blackpool, HVA]

Plate 36. A forgotten episode. Ayo Adeniye-Jones, 2nd left, with a White, Jerrims and a Lamb. Ayo was one of many Nigerian students temporarily accommodated in Hindon in the early 1930s, resulting from Edward Jerrim's West African contacts.

Plate 37. The Millennium Arch, erected over original churchyard gates,
2000 [Photo: author]

Appendix A
Hindon and District – a Chronology

878	Alfred leads *fyrd* by ?Willoughby Hedge to defeat Danes at Edington
1086	Domesday report on E. Knoyle
1184	manor of E. Knoyle sold to Winchester see (confirmed 1204)
1205	P. des Roches consecrated Bishop of Winchester
1219	Henry III grants annual fair at Michaelmas and weekly market for new town of Hindon (H.)
1220-1	H. a borough
1223-4	first H. chapel built
1331	Edward III grants 3-day fairs at Ascension and St. Luke's Day
1349	?Black Death in H.
1448	H. first sends 2 members to parliament
1458	Thomas Tropenell holds 'manors' of H. and Chicklade
1549	Reformation: H. chapel lands confiscated by Edward VI
1553	H. chapel by now dedicated to St. Luke. Chapel silver confiscated by crown. H. abounding in 'artisans'
1558	Mary Tudor establishes 'free chapel' of H. and corporation of governors
1575-1687	H. venue for JPs Quarter Sessions (VCH/W vol. 5, p.88.)
1643	Civil War : Edmund Ludlow deploys near H. before first siege of Wardour Castle
1646	E. Knoyle and H. manors confiscated from Winchester see
1/1649	Ludlow signs Charles I's death warrant
6/10/1651	Charles Stuart transits H. after 2nd battle Worcester
1659-61	Ludlow MP for H. before fleeing to France
1660	Lands restored to Winchester see

1685   4 non-Hindonians arrested in H. for joining Monmouth's rebellion

3/12/1688   William of Orange passes through H. and overnights at Berwick
            House

c. 1738   Henry Calthorpe acquires manor of H.

1748   Calthorpe Map

2/7/1754   Great Fire. 6 new bells hung in chapel this year

1760-2   turnpiking of Wilton-H.-Willoughby Hedge road

1777   corrupt election annulled

1779   George III re-charters H. Free Chapel charity. Chapel by now
            dedicated to St. John Baptist

1783   free school in existence, endowed by W. Beckford

1786   H. made centre of petty sessional division

1789   Beckford begins to buy property in H.

1790-4   Beckford MP for H.

1796   building of Fonthill Abbey begins

1797   Beckford's Twelfth Night party

1798   Masonic Lodge of Innocence and Morality 592 founded in H.

12/1800   Nelson and Hamiltons visit unfinished Fonthill Abbey

1804   H. old chapel painted by J. Buckler

1806-20   Beckford MP for H.

c.1810   Congregational chapel built in east Dene

1820s   Grosvenors buying property in H.. Angel Inn renamed Grosvenor
            Arms

1822   Beckford leaves Fonthill Abbey

1823   Beckford sells property in H. to John Farquhar

12/1825   Fonthill Abbey tower collapses

1830   James Morrison offers for Pavilion at Fonthill (completed 1838)

2/12/1830   'Captain Swing' riots: machinery smashed in H. High Street

1831   H.'s highest census return of 921

1832   First Reform Act: H. disfranchised

1836   William Gover's restoration of H. old chapel

1838   James Morrison buys Grosvenor Arms

1840   first Primitive Methodist chapel built

1844   Revised rent apportionment in lieu of tithe

1854   Hindon C of E school built

1859   Salisbury and Yeovil Railway by-passes H. to Tisbury and Gillingham

1863   High Street trees planted to celebrate wedding of Edward Prince of
            Wales and Princess Alexandra

1865   Court Grosvenor of Ancient Order of Foresters founded in H.

1867   Quarter Sessions moved from Lamb to present village hall

1868   All church property except church and yard sold

1869   H. old chapel demolished. H. becomes ecclesiastical parish

1869-1932   Croylands/Red Lion House used as vicarage

1870-1   Present Anglican church of St. John Baptist built by T. H. Wyatt

1880   last record of H. weekly market

1889   Police station and Petty Sessions moved to Tisbury

1898   New Primitive Methodist Chapel built in lower High Street

1899   Morrisons selling much property in H. including Grosvenor Arms

1909   W. H. Hudson stays at Lamb Inn

1915   last mention of H. fair in Kelly's Directory. Berwick sheep fair extinct

1921   H. Branch, British Legion (BL) founded

1922   Sale of Shaw-Stewart property in H.   Ecclesiastical parish loosely joined with Chicklade and Pertwood

1925   H. WI first founded (defunct by 1962)

1928   first piped water supply

1931   County Council takes over maintenance of pavements in H.

1934   Alterations to civil parish boundaries; Dene etc. added to H.   High Street lighting installed

1935   Wiltshire and Dorset Bus Company starts service to Salisbury

1936   Hill Terrace council houses built.

1937   H. Fellowship Club founded

1938- 1948   Wellesley House/Little Thurlow used as vicarage

1953   East St. council estate built

1953- 1988   Spero House used as vicarage

1958   Whitehill council estate built

1961   H. school becomes C of E-controlled primary school

1963   Women's Section, BL founded

1972   Final merging of 'Hindon with Chicklade and Pertwood' ecclesiastical parish. Congregational Chapel closed. School becomes C of E Aided First School

1981   Methodist Chapel closed

1982   WI refounded. Current name H. and Fonthill Bishop Institute

1984   H. and E. Knoyle schools merged into St. Mary's and St. John's School, H.

1988   H. parish part of new Tisbury Anglican Team Ministry

2000/1   H. parish part of new Nadder Valley Anglican Team Ministry

2001   Grosvenor Arms re-named Angel Inn
2003   School becomes Hindon C of E Voluntary Aided Primary School, St.
        Mary's & St. John's

Appendix B
Census Totals for Hindon

1801	793	1911	405
1811	781	1921	415
1821	830	1931	376
1831	921	1941	no census taken
1841	772	1951	477
1851	710	1961	514
1861	604	1971	534
1871	603	1981	488
1881	554	1991	493
1891	495	2001	509
1901	413		

Appendix C
Members of the House of Commons representing Hindon, 1399-1832

This list is collated from four main secondary sources:

a   a listing 'for the county and boroughs of Wilts., as given in the
        Parliamentary Return of 1872'. Transcribed by Canon FH Manley, with
        some interpolations from indentures and a Crown Office list, it covers
        the whole period (*WANHM* 47, 177-264). Early contemporary records
        are incomplete and for brevity here, years when documents are illegible

or missing, or no parliament sat are omitted. The first dates on each line are election dates. Four corrections have been made.

b   Sir Lewis Namier and John Brooke, *The History of Parliament: The House of Commons 1754 – 1790* (HMSO 1964).

c   R G Thorne, *The History of Parliament: The House of Commons 1790 – 1820*, vol. 3 (Secker & Warburg, 1986), pp. 170-1.

d   DNB entries.

There are also 13 additional entries as listed by Sheard in *The History of Hindon* (1979), for which she does not clearly state her source. These cannot therefore be checked, but the names are inserted, preceded by an asterisk.

1399	Willielmus Saltere
1448-9	Johannes Trautbek and Johannes *Rokes
1449	Willielmus Prudde and Thomas Coberly
1450	Willielmus Twynehow and Johannes Saymour
1452-3	Robertus Tylney and Ricardus Waller
1455	Johannes ?Surnour and Robertus Tylney
1459	Nicholas Hervy and Ricardus Chaundre
1467	*Sir Thomas Danvers and *Sir Nicholas Hervey
1472	Henricus Spilman and Johannes Suleard
1477-8	Willielmus Danvers and Johannes Waller
1478-83	*William Danvers
1491	*William Baynham and *Nicholas Tichborne
1529-36	Johannes Hynde and Johannes Bawdewyne
1547-52	John Story (catholic martyr) and *John Sturgion
1553-4	Willielmus Rastall and Oliverus Vachell
1554-5 or 7	Thomas Martyn and Johannes Beckinson
1557-8	Johannes Gybbon and Henricus Jones, doctors
1558-9	William Awbreye (grandfather of the antiquary John Aubrey (1626-97)) and Henry Jones
1562-3	*John Foster and *George Ackworth (of Archbishop Parker's household who was dismissed for irregularity of conduct)
1572	John Hales and Richard Polstede
1584	Ven. Dr. Dale and Richard Sowche
1586-7	John Mervin of Middle Temple and Richard Cossens or Cossyn, DCL. Chancellor to Archbishop Whitgift
1588-9	John Mervin, John Lyly and *John Thynne

1592-3   Francis Zouche and Abraham Hartwell
1597   Sir James Marvyn and Henry Jackman
1601   Thomas Thynne and George Paule (an indenture lists TT alone, another name being erased)
1603-4   Sir Edmund Ludlowe and Thomas Thynne
1620-1   John Anketill and Sir Henry Mervin
1623-4   Lawrence Hyde (the Close, Salisbury) and Matthew Davis
1625-6   Sir Thomas Thynne and Thomas Lambert
1627-8   Sir Thomas Thynne and Lawrence Hyde (of Heale)
1640 (Short Parliament) Sir Miles Fleetwood and George Garret
1640 (Long Parliament) Thomas Bennett *vice* Fleetwood, dec'd., George How *vice* Thomas Bennett, dec'd, Edmund Ludlowe, uncle of the regicide, and *?Robert Reynolds
1659   Edward Tooker and Edmund Ludlow, regicide
1660-1   Edmund Ludlow, regicide (election voided 1661) Thomas Thynne and *Sir George Grobham Howe, Bt.
1661   Sir Charles Herbert and Robert Hyde *vice* Howe, dec'd.
1678-9   Richard Howe and Thomas Lambert
1679   Sir Richard Grobham Howe and Richard Howe
1680-1   Sir Richard Grobham Howe and John Thynne
1685   Robert Hyde and Thomas Lambert
1688 (Convention) Robert Hyde and John Milner
1689-90   Robert Hyde and Sir John Berkley *vice* Thos. Chafyn, dec'd.
1695   Robert Hyde and Henry Lee *vice* Charles Morley, dec'd.
1698   Sir James Howe and Reynolds Calthorpe
1700-1   Sir James Howe and George Morley
1701   George Morley and Reynolds Calthorpe
1702   Sir James Howe and *Thomas Jervois *vice* George Morley, whose election declared void
1705   George Morley and Reynolds Calthorpe
1708   Edmund Lambert and Reynolds Calthorpe (substituted for Sir James Howe by House of Commons)
1710   Edmund Lambert and Col. Henry Lee *vice* George Morley, dec'd.
1713   Reynolds Calthorpe and Richard Lockwood
1714-15   George Wade and John Pitt *vice* Reynolds Calthorpe of Elvetham, dec'd.
1722   Henry Ludlow Coker and Robert Gray
1727   George Heathcote and Townsend Andrews

1734-41   Henry Fox, and re-elected after appt. as Surveyor General of Works

1741   Henry Calthorpe and William Steele

1747   Bisse Richards and Francis Delaval *vice* Valens Comyns, dec'd.

1754-   William Mabbott *vice* Bisse Richards, dec'd., and James Calthorpe *vice* James Dawkins, dec'd.

1761   William Blackstone and Edward Morant

1768   John St. Leger Douglas and William Hussey

1774   election declared void, see main text

1776   Henry Dawkins and Richard Smith (unseated 1777)

1777   Archibald Macdonald

1780   Lloyd Kenyon and Nathaniel Wraxall

1784-90   William Egerton and Edward Bearcroft

1790-96   James Adams, Thomas Wildman *vice* William Beckford jnr., who took Chiltern Hundreds, then James Wildman *vice* Thomas Wildman dec'd.

1796-1800   James Wildman and Matthew Gregory Lewis

1801-02   James Wildman and Matthew Gregory Lewis

1802-6   John Pedley and Thomas Wallace

1806-7   William Beckford and Benjamin Hobhouse

1807-9   William Beckford and Benjamin Hobhouse

1812-18   William Beckford and Sir Benjamin Hobhouse

1818-20   William Beckford and Hon. Frederick Gough Calthorpe

1820-26   John Plummer and Hon. Frederick Gough Calthorpe

1826-30   George Matthew Fortescue and Arthur Gough Calthorpe

1830-1   George Matthew Fortescue and John Weyland

1831-2   Edward John Stanley and John Weyland

It is noted on several early postcards of Hindon and in *Coaching Days and Coaching Ways* by W O Tristram that its seat was 'unsuccessfully contested by Lord Beaconsfield' early in his career.

This is wrong. Although Benjamin Disraeli (for this is he) considered standing for Hindon, he did not do so. He first stood unsuccessfully thrice for High Wycombe between 1832 and 1834, and once for Taunton in 1841. He was finally elected for Maidstone in 1841, but not created Earl of Beaconsfield until 1876.

Appendix D
Inns and Alehouses

Earlier studies have been bedevilled by the inability of researchers to quote sources. This note will only include summaries of documentary references seen by this writer. Allegation and hearsay are excluded. LTA = land tax assessment. WTA = window tax assessment. TA = tithe assessment, 1844. WB = William Beckford's election expenses 1812. Kelly = Kelly's Directory and predecessors. WI = WI Scrapbook, 1956. A more detailed list of these references will be placed in HVA in due course.

Angel Inn/Grosvenor Arms. See main text. 1711 lease. 1752 marriage settlement. Some LTA 1755-1772. WB 1812. TA 1844. Kelly, 1830-1939. Location: Angel Inn.

Crown Inn. See main text. Some LTA 1758-1770. Kelly 1830-1853. TA 1844. Location: P.O. May be abbreviation of Rose & Crown.

Rose & Crown. LTA 1777. WB 1812. Location: Baker's Arch (WI).

George Inn. Some LTA 1740-1781. 1759 Fricker will. 1793 sale advert Location nk.

Horse & Jockey. LTA 1750. Location: nk.

King's Arms. Some LTA 1740-1748. Location: nk.

King's Head. Some LTA 1770-1780. WB 1812. Location: site of former Methodist chapel (WI).

Lamb Inn. See main text. Some LTA 1755-1784. WB 1812. Kelly 1798-1939. Coach stage 1830. TA 1844. Location: Lamb Inn.

Malthouse. Some LTA 1761-1785. TA 1844. Probably adjunct of Angel Inn/ Grosvenor Arms, across upper High St.

Queen's Head Inn. See main text. Some LTA 1740-1784. TA 1844. Kelly: 1830-1867. Location: Apple Tree Cottage, Queen's Head Yard & Mews.

Red Lyon/Red Lion/Lyon. Some LTA 1740-1784. Calthorpe map 1748. WTA 1764. WB 1812. Applied alehouse licence 1822. Location: Red Lion House

Swan Inn. See main text. Some LTA 1750-1785. WB 1812. TA 1844. Coach stage 1830. Kelly 1791-1855. Applied alehouse licence 1822. Location: Swan House.

White Hart/Hart. Some LTA 1750-1771. Location: nk.
White Horse. Some LTA 1746-1784. WTA 1764. Location: Greystones (WI).

Appendix E
Glebe

Glebe was originally farming land or other property assigned to a priest by his patron to farm or lease out in order to supplement his main income from tithes. Sometimes such plots might be sufficiently concentrated to form a glebe farm. Ecclesiastical visitations sometimes summarize these holding in glebe terriers. These are not some extinct breed of small dog, but inventories of such land or property ('terrier' is ultimately derived from the Latin *terra*, land).

In Hindon's case it might be thought that the land assigned to support the chaplain and chapel under the grants of 1558 and 1779 were glebe, but they are not so called in the surviving documents. Glebe terriers of the mother parish of East Knoyle between 1671 and 1705[1] list no land that seems to be in Hindon, and in any case any glebe there listed must have been for the benefit of the rector. John Adams, chaplain, in replies to queries on a bishop's visitation of 1783, lists no glebe for Hindon, and a bishop's visitation of 1864 states that there is 'no glebe house.'[2]

However, an award by the Tithe Commissioners in 1872 exchanges an almost square plot at the east end of Hindon churchyard, a glebe plot belonging to the Vicar, Milles 'in right of his vicarage' with a larger rectangular plot in the south part of the present churchyard belonging to the Dowager Marchioness of Westminster.[3] This is all somewhat obscure, but a photograph taken just after completion of the new church in 1871 shows the latter area bare of gravestones. Milles' plot seems to have been taken back into the churchyard in 1931.[4]

There is a 'Glebe Farm' close to Hindon on the road north to Chicklade. Although this is now within Hindon civil parish, it was formerly part of the glebe of Berwick. St. Leonard.

Notes

1. WSRO, cat. D1/24/121-32.
2. WSRO, cat. D1/56/7.

3. WSRO, cat. 1730/20. HVA

4. PCC minutes, WSRO, cat. 1730/12.

Appendix F
Smugglers' 'Tunnels'

Such legends are not uncommon in old market towns, and in villages with substantial parish churches. They often concern supposed tunnels for the escape of recalcitrant priests, etc. etc. In most cases they prove to be drains, wide enough to send a small boy up to clean.[1]

In Hindon these legends are occasional, not universally heard of, and unknown to many who lived in the village since childhood. They appear to be mainly immigrant male fantasies.

They mainly concern belief that a tunnel could run from the Lamb's cellars west across the High Street to another cellar opposite. The survey of the Lamb's cellars has been mentioned. It found no evidence of such tunnels. It also investigated a claim that certain features suggested the top lintel of a tunnel. This was examined by freelance archaeologist Rod Brook in 2003, and found to be, literally, groundless.

In the 1730s proceeds from the excise tax on drink produced a quarter of the nation's tax revenue. After 1783 excise inspectors were full-time, paid adequate salaries, often resident locally and rotated between districts.[2] In Hindon they were resident for 30 of the 43 years between 1746 and 1811.[3] Although there is no record of their residence later, they must have visited, and it is hardly likely that they could have been unaware of the existence of tunnels.

Notes

1. S Friar, *A Companion to the English Parish Church* (Sutton History Handbooks, 1996).
2. P Clark, *The English Alehouse, a Social History, 1200-1830* (Longman 1983), p. 185.
3. Land Tax Assessments. WSRO, A1/345/215/A-C.

Notes

References are generally to the most accessible version of the information. For example, the Victoria County History/ Wilts (VCH/W) is available in the larger reference libraries in the area, and contains its own indexes to anterior sources.

Beginnings
1. H W Timperley and E Brill, *Ancient Trackways of Wessex* (Phoenix House 1965). Other trackways mentioned are also based on this work.
2. see A Burton, *The Wessex Ridgeway* (OS/Aurum Press 1999).
3. Timperley and Brill 1965, pp.xii – xiii; B Cunliffe, *Facing the Ocean* (OUP 2001), pp.55, 402-5.
4. A detailed report on the archaeology of the hill may be found in *WANHM* vol 97 (2004), pp.144-96.
5. References to barrows are from records of County Archaeologist, Libraries & Heritage Services, Wilts. CC, Trowbridge. See 'Common Abbreviations'.
6. VCH/W vol. 1, part 1, map following p.20.
7. P Salway, *Roman Britain* (OUP 1981), p.44.

Romans
1. I D Margary, *Roman Roads in Britain* (John Baker, 3rd ed. 1967), p.107; Ordnance Survey, *Roman Britain* (OS Historical Map & Guide 2001).
2. A Claydon, *The Nature of Knoyle* (Hobnob Press 2002), pp.15-18.
3. Margary 1967, pp.101-3.
4. Salway 1981, pp.618-30.

Saxons
1. J NL Myers, *The English Settlements* (OUP 1986), *passim*; R Dewhurst *The Church in Hindon* (Hindon Pub. 2000), pp.13-15.
2. Salway 1981, pp.434-45.
3. Claydon 2002.
4. A Gover, *et al*, *The Place Names of Wiltshire* (English Place-Name Soc.vol 16, CUP

1939); A H Smith, *English Place-Name Elements* (English Place-Name Soc. vol 25, CUP 1956).

5. G N Garmonsway (ed.), *The Anglo-Saxon Chronicle* (Everyman ed., 1953), E 878.
6. J Peddie, *Alfred, Warrior King* (Sutton Pubs 1999).
7. R H Jackson, 'Tisbury Landholdings granted to Shaftesbury Monastery by the Saxon Kings', *WANHM* vol.79 (1984), pp.164-77.
8. J S Davies (ed.), *The Tropenell Cartulary*. (2vols. Devizes, 1908).

Normans

1. Jackson,1984, pp.173, 175.
2. VCH/W vol. 2, p.67.
3. VCH/W vol. 11, p.85.
4. Garmonsway, 1953, E 1085.
5. F M Stenton, *Anglo-Saxon England* (OUP 1947), pp.644-9.
6. Thorn, F (ed.), *Domesday Book, Wiltshire* (Phillimore 1979). Descriptions of occupants are modernized for clarity.
7. Stenton 1947, p.276; VCH/W vol. 2, pp.182-3.
8. W H Jones (ed.), *Domesday for Wiltshire* (Longman Green 1865).
9. VCH/W vol. 11, p.85.
10. Cal. Chart., 5/6/1284.

Founder

1. E B Fryde *et al, Handbook of British Chronology* (3rd ed., Royal Hist. Soc. CUP 1986), p.72.
2. DNB; A L Poole, *From Domesday Book to Magna Carta* (OUP 1951), as indexed; M Powicke, *The Thirteenth Century* (OUP 1953), as indexed; N Vincent, *Peter des Roches: an Alien in British Politics* (CUP 1996), *passim*.

Foundation – Market

1.   Poole 1951, pp.75-7.
2. VCH/W vol 11, p.98.
3. C Cochrane, *The Lost Roads of Wessex* (David & Charles 1969), pp.106-9.
4. M Beresford, 'The six new towns of the Bishops of Winchester, 1200-55', *Medieval Archaeology* vol. 3, 1959, pp.200-3.
5. M Beresford, *New Towns of the Middle Ages* (Lutterworth 1967), p.71.
6. Ibid, p.193.
7. Ibid, p.163.
8. H A Merewether and A J Stephens, *History of the Boroughs and Municipal Corporations* (3 vols, London 1885).
9. VCH/W vol. 11, p.98.
10. Beresford 1967, p.69.
11. VCH/W vol. 11, p.98.
12. VCH/W vol. 11, p.100.

13. J Aubrey, *The Natural History of Wiltshire* (ed. J Britton, 1847), p.115.

14. *HMC, Reports of Manuscripts in Various Collections: records of Wiltshire Quarter Sessions.*

15. Poole 1951, p.77.

. . . *and Fair*

1. VCH/W vol. 11, p.100.

2. Cal. Chart. R. 1327-41, 258.

3. *Universal British Directory,* (part 3, 1794), p.269.

4. *Kelly's Directory of Wiltshire,* 1898.

5. *Kelly's Directory of Wiltshire,* 1889.

6. *Gorton's Topographical Dictionary,* 1831.

7. A Claydon, *The Nature of Knoyle* (Hobnob Press 2002), pp. 39, 83.

8. P Edwards, *The Horse Trade of Tudor and Stuart England* (CUP 1988).

9. T G F Dexter, *The Pagan Origin of Fairs* (New Knowledge Press 1930), p.9; J Chandler, *Endless Street* (Hobnob Press 1983), p.94; D K Cameron, *The English Fair* (Sutton Publishing 1998), pp.12-14.

10. VCH/W vol. 13, p.103; R Sawyer, *The Nadder: Tales of a Wiltshire Valley* (Alan Sutton Pubs 1995).

11. *Salisbury & Winchester Journal,* 28th Oct. 1833.

12. WSRO EA 158.

Hundred and Manor

1. A Gover, *et al, The Place Names of Wiltshire* (English Place-Name Soc.vol 16, CUP 1939), p.175; W H Jones (ed.), *Domesday for Wiltshire* (Longman Green 1865), p.181.

2. VCH/W vol. 4, p.328; H B Walters, 'The Wiltshire Hundreds', *WANHM* vol. 46, pp.307-8.

3. *WANHM* vol. 40, p.308.

4. VCH/W vol. 11, p.94.

5. VCH/W vol. 11, p.101.

6. J S Davies (ed.), *The Tropenell Cartulary.* (2vols. Devizes, 1908).

7. VCH/W vol. 11, p.99

8. J T Driver, 'The Career of Thomas Tropenell', *WANHM* vol. 93 (2000), pp.83-9; E F Jacob, *The Fifteenth Century* (OUP 1961), pp.462-3. H D Kitching, *A History of Maiden Bradley,* 1997, pp.15-16.

9. Davies 1908, vol. 2, pp.1-8, 12, 75.

Chapel

1. HRO 11M 59/B1/10, fiche 17.

2. VCH/W vol. 11, p.101.

3. T C B Timmins (ed.), *The Register of John Waltham, Bishop of Salisbury* (Canterbury & York Soc. 1994).

4. Cal. Pat. 1549, PRO.
5. *WANHM* vol. 12, p.370.
6. Cal. Pat. 1558, PRO.
7. Sir R C Hoare, *The Modern History of South Wiltshire*, vol.1, 1822, p.194.
8. DNB.
9. J A Williams (ed.), *Catholic Recusancy in Wiltshire, 1660-1791* (Cath. Record Soc. 1968).
10. F A Foster, *Studies in Church Dedications, or English Patron Saints* (1899); D Farmer, *Oxford Dictionary of Saints* (OUP 1997); C Joeckle, *Encyclopaedia of Saints* (Parkgate Books 1997).

Parliament to 1600

1. references for whole chapter: VCH/W vol. 5 (1957), *passim*, esp. pp.72, 111, 117, 122; VCH/W vol. 11, p.85-6; E F Jacob, *The Fifteenth Century*, pp.407, 418 and elsewhere; DNB.

17th Century

1. VCH/W vol. 11, p.99.
2. B Watkin, *A History of Wiltshire* (Phillimore 1989), pp 74-7.
3. DNB on Ludlow.
4. A Claydon, *The Nature of Knoyle* (Hobnob Press 2002), p.64.
5. A B Worden (ed.) *A Voyce from the Watch Tower: memoirs of Edmund Ludlow, 1660-2* (Camden Soc. 4th series. Royal Hist. Soc., 1978).
6. G N Wright, *Roads and Trackways of Wessex* (Moorland Pub. Co. 1988), pp.108-9.
7. *Burke's Peerage and Baronetage*, 106th ed. 1999.
8. *HMC, Reports of Manuscripts in Various Collections: records of Wiltshire Quarter Sessions.*
9. VCH/W vol. 5, p.168; G Clarke, *The Later Stuarts* (OUP 1955), pp.134-43; W S Churchill, *Marlborough, his Life and Times*, book 1 (Harrap 1947); DNB on H. Hyde.
10. DNB on Scrope Howe.
11. *Guide to St. Leonard's Church, Berwick* (Redundant Churches Fund, 1979).

Parliament – 1700-1832

1. VCH/W vol. 11, p.99.
2. Indenture of lease held in Angel Inn.
3. *Burke's Peerage and Baronetage* (2003 ed.), p.452.
4. HMC, *Diary of Viscount Perceval, afterwards 1st Earl of Egmont* (3 vols. 1922).Egmont's son was thinking of trying for Hindon, but withdrew when told that Hindon was 'a more mercenary borough than he at first supposed'.
5. Sir L Namier and J Brooke, *The History of Parliament: The House of Commons 1754-1790.* (HMSO 1964), vol. 1, p.415.

6. T H B Oldfield, *History of the Boroughs* (London 1792), p.198.

7. Sir L Namier, *The Structure of Politics at the Accession of George III* (Macmillan 1965), p.206 n.

8. H Thomas, *The Slave Trade* (Picador 1997), p.476.

9. Namier and Brooke 1964, vol. 1, p.416; C Robbins, *The 18th Century Commonwealthman* (Harvard U. P. 1959), pp.263-4, 374; T H B Oldfield, *History of Original Constitutions of Parliaments* (London 1797), pp.247-9, 413-15; O Lodge, *The Hindon Elections of 1774 and 1775* (unpublished, 1977).

10. Namier 1965, p.162.

11. T Mowl, *William Beckford, Composing for Mozart* (John Murray 1998).

12. R G Thorne, *The History of Parliament: The House of Commons 1790-1820* (Secker & Warburg 1986), vol. 3, pp.170-1.

13. WSRO. 824/2.

14. VCH/W vol. 5, pp.296-301.

Transport and Travellers

1. K G Watts, *Droving in Wiltshire – The Trade and its Routes* (Wiltshire Life Society 1990), pp.5-15. Watts has much detail on this area, but conflates Hindon Fair with Berwick Hill Fair. G N Wright, *Roads and Trackways in the Yorkshire Dales* (Moorland Pub. Co. 1985), pp.138-145; E Crittall (ed.), *Andrews' & Dury's Map of Wiltshire, 1773: a reduced facsimile* (Wiltshire Record Society).

2. Watts 1990, pp.90-1.

3. J Chandler, 'Accommodation and Travel in Pre-Turnpike Wiltshire', *WANHM*, vol. 84 (1991), pp.83-95.

4. J Copeland, *Roads and their Traffic, 1750-1850* (David & Charles 1968), p.85.

5. *Salisbury & Winchester Journal*, 15 April 1761. Fisherton Turnpike Trust Parliament Act. WSRO, A1/300/6.

6. DNB.

7. C Cochrane, *The Lost Roads of Wessex* (David & Charles 1969), pp.113-15; K Watts, *Exploring Historic Wiltshire, vol. 2: South* (Ex Libris Press, 1998), pp.72-3.

8. Cary's of 1787, Tunnicliff's of 1791 and Cary's of 1801.

9. R C and J M Anderson, *Quicksilver: a Hundred Years of Coaching, 1750-1850* (David & Charles 1973), pp.11-12, 30, 63, 121-2.

10. J H Chandler, *Stagecoach Operation through Wiltshire* (S. Wilts. Industrial Archaeology Society 1980).

11. A Bates, *Directory of Stage Coach Services, 1836* (A. M. Kelly, New York, 1969).

12. Pigot & Co's *Directory of Wilts*, 1842.

13. Wiltshire Tracts, vol. 37 (WANHS Library): Report on 1774 election.

14. Cary's *Itinerary*, 1819.

15. D Gerhold, *Road Transport before the Railways: Russell's Flying Waggons* (CUP 1993).

16. Stephen White, grandson, recollections.

17. Heather Bull, recollections.

Trade, Crafts and Phoenix, 1700 - 1830

1. Settlement on marriage of Mr. William Warne with Mrs. Mary Sharpe, 3 July 1752.
2. WSRO A1/345/215.
3. P T M Cawthorne, *Hindon, Adaptation and change in a small Wiltshire market town, c. 1720-1850* (Unpublished thesis, 2000), HVA, quoting LTAs, wills, WTAs, pp.40-42.
4. J Britton, *History of Wiltshire* (1814); VCH/W vol. 4, pp.176,178-9; M F Tighe, *Silver Threads* (Mere Papers No. 3, 1997).
5. Pigot & Co's *Directory of Wiltshire,* 1830 and 1842.
6. Research by Jonathan Steevens, London 2003.
7. P Clarke, *The English Alehouse, a Social History, 1200-1830* (Longman 1983).
8. Britton 1814.
9. *Salisbury & Winchester Journal*, 29 January 1787.
10. NMR Swindon Grade II listing notice ref. ST9132.
11. *Kelly's Post Office Directory of Wiltshire,* 1848 ed..
12. WSRO, Arch. Sarum Wills & Cons. Sarum Wills.
13. M D Anderson, *History and Imagery in British Churches* (John Murray 1971), pp.84,134-5.

19th Century: Land, Landlords, Buildings

1. M Ransome (ed.) *Wiltshire Returns to the Bishop's Visitation Queries, 1783* (Wilts. Record Soc. vol. 27, 1971).
2. Mowl 1998, pp. 60,75.
3. Readers curious about the large number of great houses in succession that have sat on the estate should see VCH/W vol 13, between pp.160 and 161, where they are all illustrated.
4. Mowl 1998, pp. 228-9; *Bath Journal*, 23 Jan. 1797.
5. DNB; *Burke's Peerage & Baronetage* (1999 ed.).
6. LTA, 1832.
7. N Sheard, *History of Hindon* (1979), who has much intricate detail of these transactions.
8. The charity survived for over 200 years, although its value diminished as the Church of England moved to a salaried system of paying clergy in the 19th and 20th centuries. It was not finally wound up until 1994, when the surviving assets were paid into Hindon PCC's account.
9. R Dewhurst, *The Church in Hindon* (2000), has fuller details.
10. R Gatty, *Portrait of a Merchant Prince: James Morrison 1789-1857* (Pepper Arden, 1977).

19th Century: Conflict and Decline

1. A G Harfield, *Capt. Wm. Wyndham of the Hindon Troop* (Soc. for Army Historical Research, 1964).
2. *Salisbury & Winchester Journal*, 4 Aug. 1794 and 13 Sept. 1830.
3. Sheard 1979, p p.27-8; Harfield 1964, p. 33; W Elderkin, *Class or Custom? Rural*

Conflict in Wiltshire : The Pythouse Riot of 1830 (unpublished, 1996).

4. Sheard 1979, p.28, quoting Beckett's great grandson A. J. Beckett.

5. E L Woodward, *The Age of Reform, 1815-1870* (OUP 1954), pp. 75-83.

6. VCH/W vol.4, pp.319,321,322.

7. VCH/W vol. 11, p.101.

8. VCH/W vol. 5, p.255.

9. Trust Accounts, WSRO A1/280/12.

10. *Kelly's Directory of Wiltshire*, 1889.

11. Dewhurst 2000.

12. Sheard 1979, p. 35.

13. *The Times.* 26 November 1963.

War

1. K Watts, *Exploring Historic Wiltshire,vol 2: South* (Ex Libris Press. 1998).

2. T S Crawford,*Wiltshire and the Great War* (DPF Pubs., Reading, 1999).

3. R Wyeth, *Warriors for the Working Day: Codford during Two World Wars* (Hobnob Press, 2002).

4. V Taylor (ed.), *The Armoured Micks, 1941-1945* (unpublished, 1997); and letter, Taylor, 6 April 2003.

5. K Wakefield, *Operation BOLERO. The Americans in Bristol and the West Country 1942-45* (Crécy Books, 1994).

6. J R I Platt,*The Royal Wiltshire Yeomanry (Prince of Wales's Own), 1907-1967* (Garnstone Press, 1972).

20th Century: Modernisation and Change

1. A bequest of James Ames, surgeon, who died in 1828 and left sacramental plate to the chapel and £10 annually to the poor. It is not clear when it was wound up, but the Charity Commissioners still listed it in 1906.

2. Sheard 1979, p.38, 43.

3. See NMR refs. Under GR ST9032 and 9132 (result of examination, not all internal, in Dec. 1985); to refs. in VCH/W vol. 4, 1959, and Sheard 1979.

4. *Western Gazette,* 9 Dec. 1988.

5. Tisbury & Mere Petty Sessions Minutes. WSRO B20 100/1.

6. VCH/W vol 5, p.328-9, and vol. 13, p.158.

7. Ransome 1971

8.   Sheard 1979, pp.35-6; J. Cawte, research 2004.

Index

Note: the appendixes and notes have not been indexed. Some incidental references to places outside south Wiltshire have been omitted. Buildings and locations are in Hindon unless otherwise stated. Towns and villages are in Wiltshire unless otherwise stated.